SUPPER IN THE EVENING

by

Al Barnes

Text Illustrations by
Bud Weert

HORIZON BOOKS

Traverse City, MI

Library of Congress Catalog Card Number: 67-26278
Manufactured in the United States of America

Printed and Bound by Harlo Printing Co.

ISBN 0-915937-01-8

DEDICATION

To my daughter, Vicki, who I hope will always remain young at heart. To my grandchildren who will find it difficult to visualize the hardships endured by those who pioneered the wilderness of the great northwest.

CONTENTS

Foreword vii

CHAPTER   PAGE

I   In The Year Of Our Lord, 1610 1

II Civil War Reaches North 7

III Sgt. Homer B. Potter, Hero 19

IV Army Of The Grand Traverse 67

V   Medical Advice Of A Century Ago 81

VI Proem 99

VII Era Of The Opera House 137

VIII Was Mother A Good Cook? 147

IX Recipes Of Yesteryear 155

X   Helps For The Kitchen Queen 161

XI Laugh, Pioneer, Laugh 169

XII The Christian Workers Came 179

XIII "A-Pioneering We Went" 187

XIV Before The Rails And Telegraph 193

XV Postal Service At The Beginning 201

XVI Wilderness Water 209

XVII An Old Settler Speaks 213

XVIII Doctor, Lawyer, Merchant, Inventor 221

XIX Century Notes 244

FOREWORD

Supper In The Evening amply demonstrates in action the author's deep conviction that "research is the key to successful historical writing."

Al Barnes, Noted Traverse City historian, writer, photographer and lecturer, has spent years doing the research which has gone into this enjoyable book. Other books by Mr. Barnes were *One Hundred Years From Old Mission* and *Vinegar Pie*.

In addition to his three historical works, he has written more than 500 articles and stories on pioneer life in Northern Michigan. A favorite lecturer in the area, Mr. Barnes has one of the largest collection of tape recordings of pioneer voices and has literally thousands of photographs and plates of regional scenes and people.

Mr. Barnes, a friendly, humorous and dedicated man, has been photographer and feature writer for the *Traverse City Record-Eagle* for 29 years. He plans shortly to retire to devote his full time to writing features, historical fiction and fact. He has lived in the Traverse City area for 35 years.

Supper In The Evening is the story of pioneer living which should be readable for anyone in any part of the country. The book contains pioneer recipes, medical advice and, in a most revealing series of letters and diaries, excerpts from a Civil War veteran who dies in action.

Illustrations for *Supper In The Evening* were done in India ink by Bud Weert, a talented and imaginative midwestern artist.

I believe *Supper In The Evening* is a highly readable and enjoyable book and I heartily recommend it.

WILLIAM G. MILLIKEN, *Lt. Governor,*
State of Michigan

Chapter I

THE YEAR OF OUR LORD, 1610

There can be no more fitting beginning for this book than one written by Mrs. M. E. C. Bates in 1904. It is the opening chapter of her own *Stories from Michigan History for Michigan Boys and Girls.* The book-length series was published in the *Grand Traverse Herald,* starting on December 22, 1904, and continuing until a total of thirty-eight chapters had been printed. Mrs. Bates loved Michigan and its Grand Traverse Region. She had beautiful mastery of the English language and her prose had the lilt of poetry.

"It was the year of our Lord, 1610. The western world, discovered by Columbus more than one hundred years before, was a new world still — a world of wild forests, lonely inland seas, great rivers sweeping on in silence to the ocean, and peaceful Indian tribes who wandered over the face of the earth, living and letting live.

"There were no cities with white-spired churches on busy streets beside the rushing rivers. No villages nestled among green hills along quiet, shaded, grasslined roads. There were no farm houses where little children played, and slept at night soothed by a mother's lullaby. It was a world of strange men and wild beasts hunting and living in the forests and along the shores of the oceans, lakes, and rivers.

"In the south the Spaniards were searching for gold and precious stones on the shores of the Gulf of Mexico and the Atlantic Ocean. They sought wealth and conquest.

"Farther north on the seaboard Jamestown, Virginia, the first English settlement in America, had just been founded and

1

stood a rude, little settlement in a clearing amid a great, unbroken forest.

"The Dutch were planning to enter and occupy the land at the mouth of the Hudson River, and did so four years later. They built the town of New Amsterdam on the island of Manhattan, now a part of the great city of New York. New England was still a wild and lonely land for it would be ten years yet before the Pilgrims were destined to land at Plymouth Rock.

"The French had, eighty years or so before, discovered the St. Lawrence River but had made no attempt at colonization. In 1608 a solitary ship sailed up the great, wide river. Its commander was Samuel Champlain, the leader in a procession that would soon enter by that river gate and take possession of the northern land. A few weeks later a cluster of rude buildings stood on the banks of the St. Lawrence, and Quebec was founded.

"All France was stirred by the news. Ship after ship came and went between the European country and the new land which had come into its possession. Those great, unknown regions where the mighty rivers swept down out of mysterious solitudes could well contain all the wonders and wealth the old world sought in the new.

"Perhaps this route was the one that, after Columbus, all the adventurers and discoverers, Spanish, French, or English, had hoped to find — the short way that should lead to China and the Indies where there might be riches untold for all who could reach them.

"There was one sure thing: All these vast regions were swarming with fur bearing animals; beaver, mink, martin, and many others. The Indians were eager to barter these valuable furs for such trifles as glass beads, scarlet cloth, iron kettles, and other items of little value in the civilized world but new to them and much to be desired.

"There were fortunes to be made in trading and many adventurous souls in France were filled, not only with desire for gain, but stirred with the delight of wild adventure. So, brave young peasant lads, glad to escape from the tyranny of the old world into the freedom of the new, or the younger members of noble families who must carve their own fortunes, came to 'New France,' as it was called, by scores and hundreds. They soon formed a class peculiar to the country and the time and were known as *'couriers du bois,'* the runners of the woods, or as *'voyageurs,'* because all travel in that northern region was by riverways in birch canoes, not by the rough and infrequent Indian trails which were the only paths in the otherwise untrodden forests.

"But there was a far stronger motive than the pursuit of wealth or the love of adventure or discovery that urged the exploration of those western wilds.

"France was a land of convents and monasteries in which monks and priests devoted their lives to penance and prayer, while in every city stood beautiful churches and cathedrals where daily incense rose from magnificent altars and the sound of chanting mingled with the chime of sweet voiced bells that swung in turret and tower. The world was full of a religious fervor unknown in the same fashion today. As the explorers sighed for new lands to discover and the fortune seekers for the wealth they hoped to find, the black robed priests desired heathen nations to convert to their own faith.

"Here their mission field was a great land, its eastern shores beaten by the waves of the Atlantic, its western boundaries lost in dim distance. Here was a race of wild copper-colored people who worshipped rudely carved stone idols, or said prayers to the Manitoes or to the spirits of the wind and the wave, the thunder and the storm. Those who would come to tell the story of the Cross came to lives of hardship and suffering. Often they came to death at the hands of the savages, who would torture before they killed.

"But soldiers of the faith came with shaven heads, cassocks of brown, black, or white, and with sandaled feet. They came with rosary and cross at side, and breviary in hand. They left their quiet monastery homes and, with eager hearts, took their way across the ocean to meet danger with devotion.

3

"From Quebec, and later from Montreal, and from the outposts of civilization, they hastened into the wilderness and wherever they could gather the red 'savages,' raised the cross and told its story to whomever would listen.

"If, after months of suffering by winter's cold in frozen, snow-covered camps, or summer days of toilsome travel through tangled swamps where insects stung and wild beasts threatened, they were permitted to baptize some dying babe, and so, as they devoutedly believed, secure its salvation, they felt amply repaid and went on their ways rejoicing.

"Here and there they established missions. These missions were to be centers from which could radiate the light of their faith.

"Of those earliest days, as far as our own state history is concerned, the records are few and faint. It is thought that in 1610 one of these missions was established near what is now Fort Gratiot. But one thing seems sure. About this time some adventurous Frenchman — it might have been pious priest or bold *voyageur* — coming out of the wilderness to the eastward saw the waters of the Detroit river flashing in the sun — who saw beyond, dim in the purple mist of distance, a fair land with green shores, groves of stately trees dotting grassy plains, the smoke curling up from Indian wigwams that clustered on the western banks, and, asking what country that might be, was told: 'It's Mischigonong, the Land of the Great Lakes.' "

Of this the Grand Traverse Region is a part.

Chapter II

CIVIL WAR REACHES NORTH

Sparsely populated though it was at the time of the Civil War, northern Michigan played an heroic part in the epic drama. The Grand Traverse Region, of which Grand Traverse County, Michigan, was a major land area, rallied to the call of the war governor, Austin Blair, with unprecedented loyalty.

In all of northern Michigan, before the opening of the Civil War, only six counties had been organized between the Saginaw valley and Mackinac. Those political divisions were: Grand Traverse, Emmet, Cheboygan, Mason, Manistee, and Iosco. The present counties of Antrim, Benzie, and Leelanau were attached to Grand Traverse County and the whole area divided into the townships of Meguzee, Milton, Whitewater, Peninsula, Traverse, Leelanau, Centerville, Glen Arbor, and Crystal Lake.

So, when mention is made of the Grand Traverse County of that early date, the area designated encompasses much more than it does today. When final figures were tabulated from northern Michigan showing the men sent to the front during the Civil War, more than half of the total came from Grand Traverse County.

M. L. Leach, regional historian of that day, said that at the beginning of the war there could have been no more than six hundred men in the Grand Traverse Region who were available, either for enlistment or draft. Despite this fact, approximately two hundred soldiers were ultimately enrolled in service. Some of this number were undoubtedly immigrants to the Grand Traverse area who came after the outbreak of hostilities.

One of the earliest residents of the region to enlist in the Union Army was Curtis Fowler, Jr., son of Curtis Fowler, Grand

Traverse County Probate Judge. Young Fowler joined the First Michigan Infantry, was wounded at the first Battle of Bull Run in July, 1861 and discharged as a result of his wound. He died March 25, 1916.

Immediately after the return of Curtis Fowler, his brother, Francis Z. Fowler, enlisted and was killed at the second Battle of Bull Run. He was the first Grand Traverse Region man to lose his life in the war. His body was returned to Traverse City and was buried at the Ogdensburg cemetery.

In mid-September, 1861, thirteen regional men volunteered their services and started for Chicago where they planned to enlist in Captain Busteed's light infantry company. Somewhere along the way their plans went awry for, in later records, it is found that some of the men were listed as members of the First New York Artillery.

Rumors circulated in the Grand Traverse Region after the group of young men left to join Busteed's outfit had a tendency to cause some unrest. Local gossips repeated the yarn that some of the Grand Traverse boys were involved in criminal activity and had been transferred to other units.

A letter from Lt. E. J. Brooks, a Traverse City man, dated February 2, 1862, set all records straight on the matter. The letter was datelined Camp California, Virginia.

Brooks went into great detail to explain why the Busteed Battery was disbanded. The whole difficulty, according to Brooks, stemmed from the theft of two horses by two incompetent officers of the battery who were later tried by a military tribunal and convicted.

The unit left Chicago by way of the Pittsburgh, Fort Wayne, and Chicago Railroad on October 1, 1862. They arrived in Washington on October 4. At that point all was well with the battery and they encamped at Camp Duncan on East Capitol Hill, which was at that time an artillery reserve and camp of instruction.

On September 2, the battery was placed under marching orders with instructions to join General Hintzleman's Division.

An order came directly from General McClellan stating that the company be declared without competent officers and the men be assigned as members of the regular artillery.

Thus, the theft of two government horses, one of which was sold for eighty dollars, caused an entire battery of men to be disbanded. Neither of the officers involved in the larceny were Grand Traverse men.

That first contingent included Martin A. Hopper, Andrew McKillip, Isaac Winnie, James Nicholson, James Fitzpatrick, William E. Sykes, Samuel A. McClelland, E. J. Brooks, Lewis Steele, Frank May, Aaron Page, Orselus Evans, and Thomas Lee. Five in this group (first five listed) were employees of Hannah, Lay and Company. Perry Hannah, in meeting with the men before they left, advised that if at any time they were pressed for funds, they were at liberty to present an on-sight draft and it would be honored by his firm.

Another group of early enlistees from the Grand Traverse Region included Hiram Odell, William Wilkes, Sidney Brown, Charles A. Lee, James Hutchinson, Jared D. Delap, A. N. Brown, Albert Powers, and M. V. Barnes.

McClellan mentioned the Grand Traverse Region soldiers in a later letter pointing out that several of them were cited for bravery during the Battle of Malvern Hill, July 1, 1862. Some of the men, including Sykes, Evans, McKillip, Nicholson, and Hopper were mentioned by name.

In October, 1861, a group of fifteen Grand Traverse Region men left Traverse City for enlistment in Grand Rapids. This contingent was headed by F. W. Cutler and included Edward Stanley, Matthew Shanley, Edward DeWaire, Andrew Anderson, Lewis Stevenson, John Williams, William Gallison, George Flack, Benjamin Rattelle, Dudley Wait, John O'Leary, Patrick Graham, George Askey, and John Rodart.

For a short period, there was a lull in recruiting in the Grand Traverse Region. Then, in the late summer months of 1862, Captain E. S. Knapp (referred to in some records as L. E. Knapp and L. Edwin Knapp), assisted by Lt. C. H. Holden,

Northport, and Lt. Jacob E. Seibert, Manistee, brought together a company of men from Grand Traverse and Manistee counties. The outfit was called "Lake Shore Tigers," sometimes referred to by the old soldiers as "The Tigers."

While Captain Knapp was engaged in securing enlistments for his company, he planned to join the 21st regiment then building at Ionia. This regiment, however, was filled before his arrival and he took his men to Kalamazoo where the 25th was also completed. Finally, the company was accepted in Jackson as Company A of the 26th regiment.

While there is no complete, accurate list of the men who left with the group under Captain Knapp, it was recorded in the *Grand Traverse Herald* that, by townships, they were: P. D. Greenman, Francis Hopper, C. R. Lackey, Horace Phillips, John A. Brainard, Milton Stites, John Duncan, Henry Odell, Oscar Eaton, and George Allen from Whitewater township. From Traverse township there were: Elias Langdon, Jr., Thomas Bates, Giles Gibson, Asa V. Churchill, and George Moody. Gilbert Lacnor and John A. Thayer volunteered from Peninsula township. From Leelanau township there were William H. Voice, Mortimer Boyes, Henry Budd, George W. Bigelow, William W. Nash, Henry Holcomb, and Charles E. Lehman.

Completing the contingent were the following from Centerville township: George Ramsdell, Joseph Warwick, Melville Palmer, William Lawson, James Lee, Frederick Cook, Jacob Hans, Deidrick White, George W. Miller, John Egler, James Adameson, L. Grand, H. Dunckelow, Thomas McCreary, Charles E. Clerk, and George Mills.

Lt. Holden, at the time of his enlistment, was prosecuting attorney at Northport and resigned his position to enter service. He served until he was honorably discharged April 4, 1864. Lt. Seibert, who assisted in enlisting the group, was killed at Poplar Spring Church, Va. on September 30, 1864.

Three men from this group, in addition to Lt. Holden, never returned home. William Voice died before he left camp at Jackson, Michigan, on September 22, 1862, less than a month after his enlistment. P. D. Greenman died at Fairfax, Va. on March 27, 1863. George Moody died at Yorktown, Va. on July 15, 1863.

It was early in the summer of 1863 that voluntary enlistments lagged in the Grand Traverse Region. Lt. Edwin J. Brooks, Northport, was endeavoring to recruit for the Tenth Cavalry, then being filled at Grand Rapids. In September of that year, Lt. Brooks was still working on a quota in an effort to beat a draft call.

Residents of Traverse township voted a bonus of fifty dollars for each volunteer credited to the township. This was the first bonus offered in the area.

When word was received in October that the draft would be made on the 26th of that same month, there was still a need for eleven men to complete the quota for the county. The board of supervisors immediately voted $1,000 as bonus money; one hundred dollars for each volunteer.

During the coming winter (1863) additional calls induced the board to increase the enlistment bonus and a special series of meetings was held to study the matter, and bonds were authorized to raise bonus money.

That the program was successful is evidenced in the records. On March 2, 1864, forty-two men left Traverse City for the Grand Rapids rendezvous.

The occasion of the departure was preceded by a community-wide party at the Hannah, Lay and Company boarding house on Bay and Union streets, known later as the Pangborn House.

The group was addressed by Perry Hannah, Morgan Bates, and Rev. J. H. Crumb. Group singing was under the direction of Charles H. Day. In keeping with the times, it was described as "soul-stirring."

In this enlistment group were the following men: Albert S. Brooks, Ernest Crain, Wm. W. Bradley, George L. Smith, Edward Beavis, Aaron Meettes, Myron A. Moody, Paul Gravel, Robert Myhill, James Lynch, Tobias F. Houghtaling, John Sutherland, Wm. W. Johnson from Traverse township.

11

James Birney Lancaster, Charles Lonkey, Columbus Winnie, Richard W. Smith, Abram D. Langworthy, Francis L. Boursaw, Wm. B. Munn, and John M. Allison were from Peninsula township; and Thomas Harmer, Adam Cook, James Manseau, Isaac Clark, James Mason, Jacob Burger, Clouve Warren, Martin Novotney, Ferdinand Dord, Philip Egler, Albert Norris, Henry Lemmerwell, James Clark, and Martin Wachall were from Centerville township.

By now — 1863-1864 — a draft was imminent. Who was in charge of the listing of eligible men in Grand Traverse county is not a matter of record.

However, among papers left by E. L. Spague, there was a draft list of men between the ages of eighteen and forty-five years. The list covered Traverse township, Grand Traverse county, and is believed to date about mid-1863.

Most common exemptions were the alien residents of the region who had immigrated from Poland, England, Ireland, or Scandinavian countries.

Indians, too, were not impressed into service, nor were those men who had served in the Mexican War or who were in federal service in another capacity.

Only a few of the possible draftees in the community were under the age of twenty years, several of them were Indians, and more still were aliens with only their first papers.

With each name on the original list was a reason why, or why not, the individual would or would not be available for service. One in particular was very adverse to war. At any rate there was a notation following the entry of Henry G. Snyder which was very brief. It was one word: "Skedaddled."

Following this call for men, the bounty in Grand Traverse was boosted, in some townships to as high as six hundred dollars. This brought one final enlistment of anything like a volunteer group. It was during the summer of 1864 (June 10) that a call was issued for twenty-three men. Within a very few days the entire quota was enrolled and headed for training camps.

In this final contingent from the Grand Traverse Region

were the following men: William Tracy, Adolphus Payette, Harvey Avery, Ira Chase, Joseph Kunn, Nelson Sherman, Edward Morgan, Ora E. Clark, William Sluyter, George Sluyter, Barney Valleau, Zodoc Wilcox, James Mason, John Reynolds, John Falrue, Leander Curtis, Alburn Atwill, Abram Adsit, Marcus Lacore, Michael Galligan, Austin Brinnon, and David Sweeney.

Of this group, Ora E. Clark was the only soldier who did not take part in the savage fighting at Strawberry Plains, Tennessee. He was on another front.

Bounty money was of considerable importance in the future of Traverse City and the Grand Traverse Region. A sum of six hundred dollars was, in those days, of considerable importance. It made it possible for a great number of the men to become land owners in their own right. Forty acres of land could be purchased for that amount and by the time the conflict was over and the lumbering industry was booming, both land and immediate revenue awaited the veteran.

Not all of the bonus money, however, was invested in real estate or other tangible property. In a letter written by Michael Stowell in 1862, addressed to his father, Joseph Stowell, then at Burr Oak, Michigan, he itemized his expenses after entering the service. Here is the list with the exception of a few minor and personal items:

$20.00 for revolver
$ 6.25 which I gave Henry for bounty [?]
$ 1.00 that I sent to mother
$ 1.50 cap
$ 1.50 silk handkerchief
$ 3.50 woolen [sic] shirt
$ .20 writing paper
$ .35 diary
$ 1.00 for knife with spoon and fork in same
$ .20 lead pencils (two)
$ .25 pain killer
$ 1.00 postage stamps
$ 1.00 repairing boots
$ .35 towel

13

```
$  .25 pocket ink stand
$  .15 bottle of ink
$  .20 envelopes
$  .25 novel
$  .25 marking my clothes
$  .50 fancy writing paper
$  .20 boot blacking
$  .20 blacking brush
$  .25 tin cup
$ 1.00 getting my certificate
$  .25 cutting hair and shaving
$  .15 pens and holder
$  .20 cough candy
$ 5.00 borrowed money from Henry Leavermore
$ 7.00 borrowed money from Jacob Whitman
```

In addition to those men from the Grand Traverse Region who enlisted with others to form a "group," many others enlisted, singly or with a companion, walking from the Grand Traverse Region to Grand Rapids or Chicago where regiments were forming. Of those, there is little record other than burials in Oakwood Cemetery, Traverse City, and in other cemeteries in the area, and the record of their membership in McPhearson Post No. 18.

In Oakwood Cemetery, Traverse City, alone, there are 246 veterans of the Civil War. Also, there is one Confederate soldier, David Duane, buried there.

McPhearson Post No. 18, Grand Army of the Republic, listed, through its years of activity, a total of 313 members. The post had a wide membership in the region and, in later years, absorbed the post at the village of Wexford. The records show that all members of that post were accepted into the local organization with full rights.

Much of the immediate quality of the conflict has been lost over the years. One of the vital links with that era, the war seen through the eyes of the enlisted man, comes from the relatively small amount of personal correspondence which has been preserved.

One such piece of correspondence, written from Ft. Blair, West Point, Kentucky, reflects the bitterness with which the soldiers viewed the enemy. While this letter was written by a Union soldier, David Beadle, whose descendants still live in the Benzie county community, it carried a consensus which certainly was common to both sides. The letter was written to his sister, Clarvina Stowell, and is his description of a clash with the enemy.

"Sunday, July 20, 1862
"Dear Sister,
"... we got back to Ft. Blair and rather glad to get back. We stayed near four weeks at the secesh city [Henderson]. We had one right smart brush with the secesh snakes. There was about 80 of us, 40 of Company B Light Artillery Musketry and 40 of the Louisville Provost Guards under Captain Dailey and Lt. Dailey.

"They attacked us about 11:00 o'clock at night in front of the brick house we were quartered in. Lieutenant Tyler, Captain Dailey, and Lt. Dailey (brothers), and two guards were at the doors and in front of the house. Lt. Z. B. Tyler was killed and the other four was wounded in the first two volleys they fired.

"Our boys fired from the upper and lower windows and doors that made them keep off this side. Then they attempted to make a rush on us and gain the building from the rear. We was ready here also to receive company.

"We think there was near 200 men of the guerillas that night. Ira's detachment and mine was on the second floor in the rear of the house. Ira had just gone below with part of his squad. I was at the head of the stairs and as I looked to the rear of us towards a graveyard covered with small trees and brush, I saw 30 or 40 of the hounds jump the fence coming for the house across a garden on the run.

" 'Here (said I) they come. Give them hell! '
"We gave them a good shot and turn from both our upper and lower batteries (as some of our boys called it). Well, this seemed too warm for them so they scud back for the brush, houses, trees, fences, and everything else that afforded them a hiding place ... they kept up a firing until nearly daylight.

"We had but one killed, Lt. Tyler, and 11 wounded, three

15

of Company B and eight of Capt. Dailey's (men) including himself and his brother. Three of his men badly (not mortally) the rest slightly.

"One of our men, G. G. Gould, in the rump . . . bullet just grazed Ira on the shoulder and one other shot through his pants. They knocked some brick chunks in my face. I paid in pills. Don't owe nothing."

The letter went on to tell of the writer being assigned to take prisoners and wounded to Louisville, and he seemed to be enjoying his duty.

News of the fighting between the North and the South was brought to the Grand Traverse Region by boat or by individuals who happened to be in one of the metropolitan areas. Thus much of the news was late in arriving and, many times, battles had been won or lost several days before details reached local people.

There was a tendency in those early days for newspapers to make capital of minor news items and stories about individual accomplishments and give slight mention to historically important items. An example of that was a short paragraph published in the *Grand Traverse Herald* on Friday, March 26, 1862. It was the account of the battle between the ironclads, *Monitor* and *Merrimac*, now an historical classic.

The paragraph read thus: "The timely arrival of the new Ericson battery *Monitor* changed the tide of affairs. She at once attacked the *Merrimac* and, after a fight of three hours, the *Merrimac* retreated into Norfolk Harbor with her sides stove in. *Monitor* was uninjured."

Announcement was made in the *Grand Traverse Herald* on Friday, July 17, 1863, of one of the few local draft calls. Enlistment in the Union Army was immediately urged throughout the Grand Traverse Region. Edwin J. Brooks, earlier a member of the ill-fated Busteed's Battery and a resident of the Village of Northport, was given authority to recruit men for a cavalry regiment.

The announcement pointed out that a draft would soon be made under the Conscription Act and those who preferred to

16

volunteer would not only be associating themselves with a crack regiment, but each recruit would receive a bounty of nearly six hundred dollars, while those who preferred to await the official call would receive no money other than their military pay.

The regiment was being assembled under the command of F. W. Kellogg, Grand Rapids, and the local quota was filled without the enforcement of conscription.

In the late summer of 1864 a regional conscription quota was announced, the last one of the war, insofar as local records are involved. Grand Traverse county, then including Benzie county, was asked for 54 men; Leelanau county, 63 men; Antrim county, 16 men; Emmett county, 6 men; and Manistee county, 34 men. These quotas were later revised downward when it was discovered that there had been an error made in the Grand Rapids office. E. C. Ladd, Peninsula township supervisor, was instrumental, by making a trip to Grand Rapids, in having the figure lowered.

On April 21, 1865, notice was given to residents of the Grand Traverse Region that the war had ended. It was an unpretentious piece on an inside page of the Grand Traverse Herald.

The brief notice was this: "General Lee surrendered the Army of Northern Virginia this afternoon upon the terms composed by myself. The accompanying correspondence will show the conditions fully.

[Signed] U. S. Grant
Lt. General"

Words will never tell the complete story of the participation of the Grand Traverse Region in the Civil War. It was a story of inspired patriotism, loyalty, suffering, heartbreak, and sacrifices.

Only a few local records and facts are still in existence, and much of the story has been lost, recorded only on simple headstones in Oakwood Cemetery and other cemeteries of the Grand Traverse Region of northern Michigan.

Chapter III

SGT. HOMER B. POTTER, HERO

The heartbreak, toil, and suffering which was a part of the Civil War is poignantly told in the letters written home by the men who fought and died.

From the thousands of letters which have been published, none show the true picture of the rebellion better than these from Sgt. Homer B. Potter. His letters and his daily diary have been preserved and edited by his grandson, C. A. Miller of Traverse City, Michigan.

The final entries in Sgt. Potter's diary have been transcribed and appear at the close of this chapter. Those brief entries portray the staunchness of character, the devotion to family and country, and the tranquility with which he accepted hardship.

"When my Grandfather, Homer B. Potter, was in the Union Army during the Civil War, he wrote to my Grandmother almost daily. Not all of the letters were saved, but those that were, cover a span of only five months of a total period of fifteen months service. It is thus quite apparent that they are only part of his correspondence and that the preceding ones were lost or destroyed.

"The letters are written in such a fine script that it is occasionally necessary to use a reading glass to make them out. The spelling is unchanged in the transcription and the words underlined are the same as in the originals. None of the letters were paragraphed, so I have supplied paragraphing for easier reading.

"I know that all who read the transcript of this correspondence will be helped in understanding, in a small way, the heartaches which Grandmother experienced and which for sixty-five years embittered one corner of her life.

C. A. Miller"

Homer B. Potter, age thirty-one, enlisted as a Sergeant in the Union Army for three years at Kalamazoo, Michigan, on August 7, 1862. He was mustered August 19th with Company I, 17th Michigan Infantry, and left Detroit August 27th for Washington, where the 17th Michigan was attached to the 1st Brigade, 1st Division, 9th Corps, General Burnside commanding.

On September 14th, less than four weeks after the regiment was organized, it was engaged in the assault at Turner's Gap, Maryland; and it took part in the Battle of Sharpsburg (Antietam), the bloodiest single day of the war, where he was wounded September 17th after having been a soldier only twenty-nine days.

He was invalided home and when his wound healed, one arm was partially incapacitated. He rejoined the army and was transferred to the quartermaster corps, but he pined for his old regiment and was allowed to rejoin it. He was back with his company when they crossed the Rappahannock during the Battle of Fredericksburg, without coming under fire.

The 9th Corps was one of the units which was sent West to join Grant's army and on February 14, 1863, the 17th Michigan left Aquia Creek, Virginia, for Newport News. From there the regiment went by boat to Baltimore, by rail to Louisville, and by rail thirty-five miles southwest to Bardstown, Kentucky.

On April 3rd the troops moved thirty miles southeast to Lebanon, Kentucky, then thirty miles south of Lebanon to Columbia, finally marching to Jamestown, Kentucky, twenty-five miles from the Tennessee border on May 31st. At this point plans were changed, for on June 4th the troops returned to Louisville, going from there by rail to Cairo, Illinois, then by boat down the Mississippi to take part in the Vicksburg campaign. On June 14th they went ashore at Memphis, where the first letter was written.

"Memphis Tenn. Sunday June 14th, 1863

"This is very dirty paper but it is the best I can do. I am seated in a beautiful park one square block from the river. Our reg't was ordered to go ashore with side arms (belt and bayonet) and were marched into this park and dismissed for a few minutes. Where we shall go then I do not know, perhaps to church. There is a church bell ringing now.

"I mailed a letter to you Friday night. When I wrote, we were just above the city taking on coal. Well we lay there all night and about 8 o'clock yesterday morning went back to the landing and stayed there until 1 o'clock in the afternoon when we run up the river again about ½ mile and all went ashore with our arms and baggage in the woods while the boat was cleaned, during which time myself and 4 others went about a mile upstream to look for blackberries. We crossed a small channel onto an island but found none. We stopped at a house and got some milk to drink for which they would take no pay. The man said he had only 11 acres of land but he paid one hundred dollars an acre for it.

"The timber here is principally cotton wood. Some of it grows very large. It looks a good deal like white wood. The cotton grows in small pods on the twigs. I will send you a specimen of the cotton and pods as I picked it up. In some places the ground is nearly covered with it. It does not seem to be any warmer here than in Michigan. I have seen it much warmer there at this time than it now is here. In the center of this park is a statue of General Jackson. On one side of the pedestal is inscribed the words of the old hero; 'The Federal Union; it must be preserved.' Some villanous traitor has tried to scratch out the word 'Federal.' I would like to get my fingers on his breathing apparatus. I would never let go until his every nerve and pulse was still.

"What horrible writing. My pen is poor and my ink, which I bought at Cairo, seems to be bad also. What we are laying here for is more than I can tell: all kinds of reports are circulated.

"It is said there is forces enough at Vicksburg. I suppose more or less fighting is now going on there. We are hourly expecting to hear of the capture of the place — I am so sleepy I cannot write. I think I will walk around some. Well I have been around town some and am now on board the boat again. I passed

21

the military prison. It is a very large building, and I was greeted as I passed by the ugly visages of a number of our southern brethren. There is some prospect now of moving. I think they are getting up steam. Tell Frank there was several pet squirrels playing in the trees in the park.

"I have now gone on shore to see a little about our supper, which is being cooked. I guess I will close and hand this to some-one to mail for me. We may go soon or we may not but I think you had rather have a short letter now than to wait 2 or 3 days longer for a long one. There is a great amount of cotton here which belongs to the government I suppose. There are 30 heavy guns laying along the bank which were taken from the Rebels when this place was captured. I have just been and examined most of them. They range from 34 to 64 pounders, and are marked CSA. I saw 2 that was spiked. Darling, hereafter direct letters to Cairo instead of Louisville. I am very anxious to hear from you. Kitty, take good care of yourself and the little ones, and keep up your spirits and be cheerful. Goodbye Love"

"Steamer Leonora Monday June 15, 1863
"My Dear Wife:
"I am very well. I am seated on the bow of the boat with my feet hanging over the water. To my right is Arkansas, and to my left Mississippi. It is a beautiful morning. We are just passing a very small village on the Mississippi side, the other shore is all woods. In some places the river is skirted with a small growth of cottonwood, standing so thickly that it would be difficult for a person to get through it. We met a steamboat a few minutes ago. The "Ike Hammatt" and now are about meeting another having two coal barges in tow. It is the "F. Wilson." I can see some of the dangers of navigating this river. There are a great many snags, four are in sight now. They are logs and trees, which float, until finally they sink enough for part of them to become embedded in the sand. The channel is also continually changing, washing away the banks in one place, and filling up in another so that where a boat may go today it

may not a month from now; the banks are washed away sometimes for miles taking trees, fences, and buildings and forming sand banks in other places which are soon covered with young cottonwood, which grows very rapidly. We have just passed the mouth of a large stream, putting in from the Arkansas side, but I cannot say what it is.

"I mailed a letter to you last night at Memphis in a great hurry. I guess you will think I commenced it in a very abrupt manner. I am ashamed of it. It is the last you will see of that style. I was on the upper hurrican deck, writing, about 6 o'clock when the bell rang and whistle blew, and I hurried down and barely had time to hand it to a citizen when the boat shoved off. I mailed a letter to you at Lebanon containing 10 dollars, I mailed another at Cairo, and 2 at Memphis.

"The river above mentioned is the St. Francis. We are now approaching the city of Helena, Arkansas. It is a small town on ground that is frequently overflowed, as I see by the wrecks of several scows that have been washed into the suburbs. There are high irregular bluffs in the rear, we have a large force lying here. There is a gun boat anchored in the river with guns run out. There is a Negro reg't encamped on the bank. There is also one at Memphis and, by the way, the blacks prove to be our best soldiers to fight, notwithstanding all that the Copperheads say to the contrary. There are now 4 boats behind us and 1 ahead, all loaded with troops. We have just met a steamer loaded with cotton, convoyed by a gun boat.

"I forgot to send the cotton in my last letter, which I mentioned, and even had I not forgotten it, I had not time. I have got also 2 branches of regular cotton, just as it come from the pod, which I mean to send so that you may see how the seed grows. You can readily tell it from that which grew on the cottonwood. I will send both in this, if I have an opportunity and do not forget it. I got some creeper peas, at my friends at Lebanon, which I will send soon. They grow from 4 to 8 inches high and by planting a few every 8 or 10 days, we can have peas all summer.

"We sailed last night until 9 o'clock and then stopped until daylight this morning. How *glad* I should be to hear from you. Darling, if I was at home, seated by a stand, with a good pen, I believe I could write better. Besides my inconveniences, the boat trembles so that it keeps me in a constant tremor. I fear you cannot read it.

"6 P.M. We are now lying up to shore on the Arkansas side. We have been here about 2 hours. When we arrived, there were 3 gunboats lying here, which has stopped everything coming down, for what purpose I do not know. There are now here 7 steamboats and several barges loaded with hay and coal. A steamer is now coming up the river. Since we stopped here, one of our men has caught a fish of the *cat* order weighing about one hundred pounds and measures nearly 3 feet in circumference. While they were pulling him in, a still larger one showed himself above water with a splash. It is clouding up in the southeast and looks as though we might get a shower.

"Tuesday morning. We are all (5 boats) sailing together accompanied by a gunboat (an ironclad) which are very plenty here. We have just met one going up. We started at daylight. It is a splendid morning and a pretty sight to see our fleet sailing down the river, which is quite a brook. I went ashore last night on Arkansas soil to see about cooking our supper. We boiled potatoes and made coffee. I went with several others back into the woods a short distance. The ground is covered with driftwood. The country here is sometimes overflowed for miles, and pretty deep too judging by marks on the trees. It did not rain much last night, but sprinkled a little; not enough to disturb us. I sleep on the hurricane deck with the heavens for a roof.

"Afternoon. Last night soon after I got asleep I was roused by picket firing. We were soon under arms and expected an attack, but it did not come. The pickets probably got frightened at something. All went well today until about 9 o'clock. Our transports kept close together, the gunboat bringing up the rear. About 9, we saw a boat lying ahead of us, and on approaching, found it to be a gunboat. Before we got to it, we (or the

24

forward boat, rather) received a volley of musketry from the woods on the Arkansas shore. Both gunboats instantly opened on them and shelled the woods some 20 minutes. We run about a mile and stopped. We could see none of the guerillas, or at least I did not. They did not shoot after the first volley, which I should judge was about 20 shots, which did not reach the boat. There was considerable firing from the boats, but the shots all fell in the water. The gunboat that came down with us left us here and the other went in advance, firing a shot or two occasionally, but has just left us and gone back, having probably passed all danger.

"Sundown. About 3 hours ago there came up a thundershower and the wind blew a gale. We undertook to land and were driven onto the shore and broke the water wheel considerable, not so bad, however, but that we are running again as fast as before. We are now having a pleasant sail. So you see we have had a battle (?), a storm, and a shipwreck today. A young man of Co. H. was accidentally shot today. He was on guard at the top of a flight of stores leading to the 2nd deck. He was sitting and reading and his gun slipped down, and the lock struck a step with force enough to explode the cap. The ball passed through his body lodging in the skin on his back. It is not expected that he will live.

"Wednesday morning. It is somewhat cloudy and cool. It rained some in the night. We are now on the Louisiana shore and have just passed another Negro reg't. We expect to land about 10 o'clock 10 miles above Vicksburg.

"Now Darling, do not be at all anxious about me. I am as safe here as at home. Give me your prayers and *we* will trust the Lord implicitly. I shall take good care of myself, and you must do the same. The man who was shot yesterday is dead. Tell Frank to be a good boy so that I can hear good news about him. All is *very* well. Give my love to the friends. I long *so* much to hear from you. Goodbye Kitty. Your affectionate husband: H. B. Potter

"I shall write often. If you do not get letters regularly,

25

do not be alarmed. They have a long distance to go. Kiss the little girls for me. How glad I should be to hear from you all."

"Rear of Vicksburg, Thursday, July 2nd, 1863
"My Dear Wife:
    "I am very well and all goes well. I mailed a letter to you yesterday. I am sorry I have not got a better pen. You need not think I have used up all the paper I brought from home. It is in my carpetbag with the officers baggage and has not come up since we moved last. We rec'd a mail last night. I do not expect another until tomorrow. Vicksburg still holds out or did this forenoon, for the firing was heavy. We do not hear any now. Nothing but a miracle can save them.
    "I went after berries this morning and found the best I ever saw. I eat until they neither looked or tasted good. Pineapples grow here. Some of our men went out on fatigue duty today, probably digging rifle pits. It is the first work we have done since we moved. It has been a warm day. I will tell you how high the sun is at noon. When I stand with my face to the North with my hat off, the shadow of the top of my head is about 10 inches from my toes. It looks very much like rain tonight. I think everyday when I have such good times, how anxious you must be about me thinking probably that I am in that battle or series of battles at Vicksburg. But you need fear no longer. We never have seen the time since we have been in the field when we have been so much out of danger as at present; and I guess if you could see me, you would think I looked healthy.
    "Friday P.M. It is cloudy and cool, and the cannonading is fearful. I have been sleeping and have just waked up. I picked about a quart of beautiful berries today which I eat with sugar. Another fort was blown up last night and 20 deserters came *within our lines.* They give doleful accounts of the condition of the besieged. The general who now has command of our corps says we shall go back to our department in less than two weeks. He said this 3 days ago. It may be that the fall of Vicksburg is

26

to be the condition, but they cannot possibly hold out many days longer. There are many horses and mules brought in by our men, which are turned over to Uncle Sam. Some of our men have been 8 or 10 miles after them. Yesterday a *grindstone* was brought in and a few days ago a large grapevine chair. We have used all the pork, mutton, and beef we could find. That is how we guard rebel property. There is now a thundershower coming up in the east, and there is a thundershower of a different nature at Vicksburg in the west. We have got another substitute in our company. From such good Lord deliver us.

"Saturday, July 4th, P.M. Good news, Darling: Vicksburg surrendered at 7 this morning! but you will get the news long before this reaches you. Men who were on guard last night say that about 2 o'clock a battery of very heavy guns opened and fired very regularly about one a second for some hours. They fired very sharp until this morning about 7 and I have not heard a gun since. There, the woods are ringing again with cheers. Some more news probably. Kitty, of course you will rejoice with us. We understand there was 27,000 prisoners taken and 20 thousand stand of arms, but be this as it *may*, I *think* there is no doubt of the fall of the city. I have drawn 3 days rations and we are to be in readiness to march. Probably to our old camp and then to the landing. I should like very much to see Vicksburg but do not expect to.

"We rec'd no mail yesterday. I hope to get a letter today. Darling, you can send anything to me at any time for it will follow the regiment wherever it goes. It is a very quiet Fourth with me but a happy one nevertheless on account of our success at Vicksburg. We are going now, Darling, and I will mail this if I can. I am very well. Goodby Darling. Love to all. Your affectionate husband: H. B. Potter

"P. S. Sunday morning. I could not mail this yesterday. We *marched* through clouds of dust about 6 miles towards the Black River and camped just after dark on an old camp ground of an Ohio reg't, I think, in the woods which to all appearances has been very recently deserted. Several chairs were there, one nice

27

sofa rocking chair. There is a nice bedstead in use here and a stand. They came from a planters house close by. Some of our company went over this morning and got relics, among which were some books. One of them got a grammer marked Mary E. Young. I went afterwards but there was nothing left, there was 10 *nigger* shanties around the house which were all desolate. There was also a cotton gin on the plantation which I visited. I expected we would start early this morning but I see no prospect of moving yet.

"Vicksburg *is* taken, Kitty, and 27,000 prisoners and near 300 pieces of artillery including about 90 heavy siege guns. That is glory enough for one Fourth of July. I have been over to our Southern brothers house again and got some beans for dinner. There were perhaps 20 bushels there. I have got a relic now *sure* if I can carry it. It is a Bible *dictionary*, just what we want. The man who got it sayed he would not carry it and I think I shall try to carry it. It *will* make a pillow by night and good reading matter by day. If I could succeed in getting it home, I would not take 10 dollars for it.

"Monday morning. We moved about 3 miles last night and camped in the woods again. We rec'd a mail yesterday but I did not get that letter. How I wish I could hear from you. I shall believe that you are getting better or at least no worse. I hope I can mail this today for I want you to hear from me frequently if I cannot get your letters regularly. We are very much encouraged about the prospect of the war closing. Every day looks brighter. We are in the very best spirits. We are pressing the enemy to the wall. We are now near 2 miles from the Black. The country here is not so very hilly and broken as it is near Vicksburg. There is thousands of acres of corn here, of the best kind. But one man planteth and another reapeth. The mail will not go out until night. Our postmaster came up yesterday.

"Tuesday morning. I am *very* well. We had a shower last night. We moved up to the river last night and are building a bridge. We rec'd a mail last evening. Why don't I hear from home. I shall mail this this morning, should before if I had a chance. How does Frank get along with his studies? Goodbye Darling. Homer. I enclose 5 dollars."

"Rear of Vicksburg, Miss. Saturday, July 25, 1863
"My Dear Wife:
"I mailed a letter to you yesterday and enclosed a secesh letter. I have another which I will send soon. I received your *precious* letter of the 10th night before last. I was never more rejoiced to hear from you, it brought such good news, though I knew you would get better, and I know that your health will continue to improve. How do I know? Why I have asked our Father and so have you and I *dare* not doubt. I have just written to Mr. Guernsey. I told him he could go on with the house for it really ought not to stand so. I told him I had always done as well as I could by him and hoped he would do so now by me. I shall probably never be able to do the work myself. Darling, we shall soon occupy it. May the Lord hasten the time.

"We have an abundance of rations now. I drew beans and potatoes. The potatoes are cut fine and dried. We are on the opposite side of the road from our old camp and get water to another spring, as beautiful as I ever saw, *very* clear and pure. We have a nice shady camp and are fast recovering from the effects of our march. *I am very well.* We are waiting for boats to take us up the river. We shall all be overjoyed to get back north, where it is not so warm, and where we can get mail more readily. I have just been to dinner, we had bean soup. I had pancakes last night and this morning. Mr. Hess, Mr. Snow, and myself stay together. We bought 5 pounds of flour yesterday for 25 cts. Mr. Snow has a frying pan. Oscar Hall of Kalamazoo is dead. We rec'd the news yesterday.

"Kitty, can't you see me. I am here in this ravine in the shade, reclined on my elbow, writing on my Bible dictionary which is lying on the ground, and little specks of sunshine are playing over the paper. About 8 rods from me is the *well* beaten *path* to the spring. Men are constantly passing but seldom one seems to notice me.

29

"Evening. I have been bathing and washing this afternoon. Mr. Snow is getting supper while I write. We have fried pork, flour gravy, pancakes, potatoes, and peach sauce.

"Sunday morning. It is a beautiful Sabbath and is really quiet in camp. How I wish I could spend my Sabbaths at home. There has been another change in brigades. There were formerly but 3 brigades in our division. The 4th is now formed consisting of the Michigan 8th, New York 79th, and our two capital regiments. There has been conflicting rumors here about the rebel Lee, but all concede that he has been roughly handled. It is now said that he has got back into Virginia, but I do not believe it. I think that his raid North was the worst thing he could have done for his cause. It seems that the devil has taken him or the Confederacy, rather, as far as he wishes to and is now leaving them to their own distruction. We have reports through rebel sources that Charleston is taken. I hope it is so.

"One day at Jackson when our regiment was skirmishing, the day those 2 Potters were wounded, there was a flag of truce for an hour. Our men and the rebels met between the lines, shook hands, traded knives, canteens, belts, and etc. They gave our men some tobacco. They were very tired of the war but an officer said they would never come under the Stars and Stripes. Poor souls, they will be obliged to. Some shook hands at parting, then every man to his post. How strange!!! I was sorry I could not go. I was asleep or nearly so at the time until the time was so 'exhausted' that it was unsafe. Sergeant Fisher of our company and myself were in our proper position 10 paces in the rear of the skirmish line. I had been having the toothache all day and a little of a nervous headache. I had lain down and just got into a drowse when he left to go and see the rebels. When he returned and told me, I started instantly but it was so late I dared not go. I was sorry.

"The country here is full of paroled prisoners, who declare that they have seen enough, and will fight the U.S. no more. Hundreds at Vicksburg refused their paroles but preferred to take the oath of allegiance. It looks hard to see the desolation

30

that our army has made in this state but secession called us down here and war is a stubborn reality. We have captured hundreds of horses and mules, harnesses, saddles, carriages, carts, and wagons. We have driven off and used cattle, hogs, sheep, turkeys, geese, ducks, and chickens, and found in *many* places barrels of sugar and molasses. Their houses which are generally built without much taste are richly furnished, all of which was left when the owner fled, only to be broken up and spoiled. At each house seems to have been a very large and well selected library. These were carried off by those who like books and if I could have had 2 wishes, the second would have been that I could send home as many books as I choose. It made me feel sad to see hundreds of volumes trod underfoot. Rich pianos were found in the house for soldiers — *Yankee soldiers* to thump on, crockery and glassware was carried off, and rich furniture knocked to pieces. Along the roads and scattered through the woods were nice chairs and sofas, where guards and pickets had been stationed, and large and beautiful mirrors were hanging on trees. There is a war picture for you, how do you like it?

"Monday morning. It is cloudy and cool. It rained much yesterday afternoon which prevented my writing. I want to mail this today and consequently cannot write so much as I otherwise should. But I shall soon send another. It rains very hard here generally when it does rain. I cannot prove who it was in our company who threw away my coat, nor do I know who carried it off. The man who found my Bible and letters got them on the ground where the coat had lain. Darling, you need not send any scissors for when I get to civilization, I mean to get another razor and take care of it.

"Mrs. Sect paid quite a tribute to our little one I think. I will come and see her soon and tell you what I think of her. What is her other name to be. I am *so very* glad — happy to hear that you are gaining, that your nerves are a little stronger, that you can rest better nights, and that you can *sing*. Kitty, be cheerful and hope on, and you will do well, and especially continue to take Dr. Prices medicine until you are *perfectly* well.

31

Never mind the cost. This is my especial wish. I sing a good deal. That Bell does not come.

"Darling, if you think it advisable, will you tell Frank that I should like to have him write me a little letter and I will answer it. I think it would have a good effect. Mr. Snow wrote 2 small letters to his children yesterday. I think Sarah means to make thorough work of her education before she commences to teach. Well that is right. Our clothing has come and I have drawn a pair of shoes, pants, haversack and canteen. I suppose Lil's husband has gone over to his Southern friends. I hope she will enjoy her journey. It seems strange to hear that of her. I hope soon to hear *good news* of you, and shall be very glad when you can write all you want to. My love to our friends. The Lord bless you with peace, health and prosperity, is the prayer of your affectionate husband: H. B. Potter

"Enclosed is a secesh envelope. I send another secesh letter. Notice the date. We had just driven them across the river."

[The first part of this letter was missing.]

". . . being so fierce. Many had been out and got bread and biscuit and potatoes and Mr. Snow had bought a little meat. We could not get any more rations until tonight, and not then unless the wagon train came up. I went with a man by the name of Wright. We had not gone far when our brigade left in a hurry, but of course we knew nothing of it. No one thought we would move until today. We went back on a back road from house to house finding nothing, but being told in each case at the next house we would be likely to get something. After going 2 miles and resolving to go no further, the lady told us that Mrs. Nolan lived about a mile furder on and she reckoned we could get all we wanted *thah*. She seemed so positive that we took courage and went on but when we got *thah*, *her* flour had been all baked for the soldiers and she could not even get us a dinner, but I finally persuaded her to give us a little something for we had walked until we were hungry, so she stired up 2 or 3 black girls to help her and about 3½ o'clock we sat down to warm corn bread, chicken, bacon, sweet potatoes baked and coffee for which she said she had paid 6 dollars a pound Confederate money. Her husband had been a Union man but was pressed into the rebel service and was at Vicksburg when that place surrendered, but had been sick some time in consequence of which he was discharged and died 8 days after reaching home. While we were eating, another lady came in whose husband had been pressed into rebel service and is now a prisoner.

"Well, we returned to camp and found our things all right, a guard having been left with them, there was so many out. We went to the depot and found that our brigade had gone to Greenville 30 miles northeast, except the Michigan 2nd. I concluded to go on the next train with them and found Harvey Seymour. I afterwards learned that our Quartermaster with 12 or 15 of the 17th men were at the depot, and I took my things and went to stay with them. Two trains had gone with troops and about 10½ o'clock one train returned bringing back part of our brigade. They told us that all had been ordered back. By a telegraphic blunder we had been ordered to Greenville instead of Knoxville. In about an hour the 17 came along on another train and I got on board. It was a bright moonlight night and I rode on the top of the cars. It was 45 miles to this place, the road passing through splended country under a good state of cultivation. It is more rolling than the land in Michigan. The corn crop is heavy, and we have driven the rebels out just in time to save perhaps a million bushels. We arrived here just before daylight.

"Afternoon. We have moved into camp about 1½ miles from the depot. We have got our tent pitched and our bunk built and I have but a few minutes to write. The mail leaves at 4 o'clock. We have had no opportunity to send out mail since a week ago today. It is said now that we will get mail 3 times a week by way of Nashville and Chattanooga. We are in high spirits, Burnside is sweeping everything before him. He is moving northeast and when we came from Morristown, we were going right away from him. We are pleasantly situated, within speaking distance of a large river, and have one spring capable of supplying 20,000 men. It would turn a small mill. I have not been in to town but it appears to be a nice place of 15,000 inhabitants. It is rumored today that Rosencrans has driven Bragg and captured 12,000 prisoners. Our men were told up at Greenville that the rebels were nearly frightened out of their senses. They are coming in by hundreds and giving themselves up.

"I am very well. Tell Frank I expect to hear good news from him. Give my love to all our loyal friends. Do you read any of my letters to Uncle. I wish you would; such portions as you see fit. Goodbye Darling. Your affectionate husband, H. B. Potter."

"Knoxville, Tenn. Saturday morning, Sept. 26th, 1863
"My Dear Wife:
"I am very well. I mailed a letter to you yesterday, the first I have had a chance to send for a week. As I told you in my last, we are pleasantly situated on the bank of the Holston River, which is here very large. In front can be seen the Smoky Mountains 50 or 60 miles distant. The ground here has been used for a camp, perhaps ever since the war commenced, for some 20 acres is trod nearly as hard as a highway. No doubt tens of thousands of rebels have camped here. The citizens generally seem very glad to have us come here. The rebels are coming in by hundreds and giving themselves up. Yesterday a full company of cavalry came into this town. Gen. Burnside's headquarters is here. The people through this part of the state think everything of him. A rebel deserter from Richmond came down on a train yesterday on his way home. He said if we wanted to take Richmond without much loss, all we wanted to do was to wait awhile and they would all desert. We are preparing for another expedition but it will be only to drive the rebels like lost sheep and take prisoners. I am anxious to hear from Charleston. We get no news at all.

"We have soft bread here, warm from the oven. Butter is only 60 to 65 cents per pound. We have fresh beef every day. The woods are full of black walnuts, chestnuts, some butternuts, and worlds of what is called chickapins. These are a species of chestnut and taste much like them. They are shaped about like an acorn and about ¾ as large. They grow on bushes in clusters about like hazelnuts. There are thousands of bushels through here. There is also many PawPaws and hickory nuts. I think I shall wash some this afternoon.

"A year ago now I was on my journey home. We have orders to be ready to move at a moment's notice, and I shall defer washing for today. I think I will now write a short letter to Mary. We are to have regimental inspection at 5 o'clock. It is now 2. I do not think we shall move today and I will finish this if I can and mail it *if I can.*

"Afternoon. I have just mailed a letter to Mary and as I have a spare minute now, I will write again to you. Inspection will come off in a few minutes and I shall have no more time tonight to write.

"Sunday P.M. It is a pleasant day. I took a squad to church this morning. We went to the Baptist Church, a neat brick building. Sabbath school had just commenced. We occupied 2 slips, and the superintendent asked a chaplain to entertain us. We were furnished with Testaments and for our lesson, took the first part of the first of St. John. We had an interesting time. The school was the smallest I ever saw, there being but one class of children, and small Bible class of adults. I liked the appearance of the superintendent much. There was preaching (?) at 10 o'clock. I did not like the looks of the minister. His text was the 2-3 and 4th. verses of the 7th. of Daniel. It was a dry historic oration of the rise and glory of Babylon. There was no Christ in it, no practical piety, and no application. The congregation was small and about one half soldiers. They had congregational singing. The people here seem much more enlightened than those in Kentucky.

"I am told the mail does not go out from here at all now. If so, we shall not get any mail. I do not think it is so for a few scattering letters came to our reg. yesterday, which came in the mail of the 23rd. Corp. I shall put this in the bag as soon as I finish it anyhow. 2 brigades of our division are ordered it seems

35

to march tomorrow morning at 8 o'clock, with 8 days rations, but we have no orders and it is said that we are going to stay here for the present.

"10 o'clock P.M. I can write but little more tonight for I have but ½ inch of candle and we are to be called up at 3 in the morning and march at 5, and perhaps I can leave this so as to mailed here.

"I have just received your *precious* letter of Sept. 11th. Oh how thankful I am to get it and hear that you are all doing so well. I am very sorry that Ma was sick, I trust she is better now. *Thank you*, Darling, for those nice flowers from *our own* garden. They still retain their colors. I shall keep them. I hope you will not have to give Nettie much quinine. I am sure I cannot say what will be done with our things. I do not think Mr. Hollister will let them get damaged. I wish you would write to Mary to see him, and tell him I will pay him well for his trouble if he will care for them. My candle is going. Goodnight, Kitty.

"Well, I guess I will write a little more by firelight. I am anxious to write a little more and mail this in the morning if possible. I think I have heard that Knoxville is taken. It is also true that we hold Chattanooga. But it is a mistake about Burnsides resignation. The old hero will fight to the end of the war, if he lives.

"Tell Ma I want to hear from home oftenest when there is sickness there. Now, Darling, if you do not get letters from me often, do not be alarmed for we are "Flying" through country where mails cannot be relied on. Whenever you wonder how *I am, I am well and doing well.* I shall write every day that I can, and mail letters every opportunity. We have just got word from the Quartermaster that we shall not go before noon tomorrow, and perhaps not until next day, and I hope to write more in the morning. I received a letter tonight from Thomas. He is well. I hope to meet him soon. He was but 14 miles from Chattanooga when he wrote, and I suppose we go to that place. I will send his letter with this.

"Monday morning. 8 o'clock. Well, after receiving orders

36

to march and having them countermanded, we were finally called up at 3½ o'clock and started without any breakfast. We marched to town and then to the river to cross. Here we lay until sunrise, waiting for a battery, and one regiment of infantry to cross on 3 skows. After crossing, we waited about ½ hour for the remainder of the brigade (2 regiments) to cross. Before crossing the companies all made coffee but just as we commenced eating, we were ordered forward and I finished my breakfast while crossing. We then marched a mile from the river and turned into the woods and stacked arms. We now have a chance to make coffee again if we wish to and finish our meal. I do not know whether we go any further today or not.

"Tell Frank I went to Sunday school yesterday and there was but one class of children. Tell him I go to SS every chance I have. I am very sorry I could not go home, and most of all for your disappointment. But, Darling, the war will soon be over and when I get home, we will be glad that I did not go now. I will soon come and eat that lunch. Now, Kitty, if the intervals between my letters are very long, do not be anxious about me for I shall be well and safe all the time. As soon as I find that my letters reach you, I will send you some more money. I suppose you received the five dollars in my letter of the 8th. although you do not mention it. Now, Kitty, be very careful and prayerful, and trustful, and cheerful. Give my love to all my loyal friends. Goodbye Dear. Your affectionate husband: H. B. Potter"

"Knoxville, Tenn. Thur., Oct. 1st, 1863
"My Dear Wife:
"I am very well; always well. I mailed a letter to you day before yesterday, though I suppose it did not go out until yesterday morning. I intended to have written to you yesterday, but first noon and then night came before I was aware of it. I wrote a letter to Thomas which with my usual duties seemed to use up the day. When I closed my last letter to you, we were lying about a mile south of town in the woods expecting to go back to our old camp. We are still here in the woods but have gone into

camp, that is, laid out streets and pitched our tents. We have got a beautiful grove with no underbrush, on the top of a long ridge about one hundred feet above the valley each side, extending east near one half mile to the road. We are on the west end of it. Thus we have a steep hill all around us except towards the road. We have cleared the old leaves from the ground and burned them. We have good water on both sides of us but we have to carry it up a long steep hill.

"Of course, I cannot say how long we will stay here. Colonel Poe, who commanded us at Fredericksburg, is Topographical Engineer here and he is doing all he can to have our brigade stay here. It was rumored yesterday that Rosecrans was badly whipped and the rebels were approaching us 60,000 strong. This caused a nervous sensation on *a few* fainthearted weak kneed ones, but nearly all discredit it and pay no attention to it. I do not think you will ever hear of the rebels attacking the 9th Army Corp. They fear us as they do death. Burnside telegraphed to General Park (who commands this Corp.) before we left Crabb Orchard to bring his old Corp to Knoxville even if there was scarce a man fit for duty. He said that the public announcement that the 9th Corp. was here would be sufficient to keep the rebels at bay.

"Charles Mench has just made me a visit. He is well, hearty, and in good spirits. His regiment is lying ½ mile from here just across the road. He says they too are in the woods, entirely hid from view from the road, but they have not so nice ground as we have.

"Darling, understand that no considerable force of the enemy can approach us until they have driven Rosecrans from Chattanooga, which they never will do. We understand that the rebels have evacuated Charleston and given up Virginia, and are massing their forces to oppose Rosecrans. But Grant is approaching to help him, and the government can send 40,000 a week to him. The rebels are deserting faster than they were ever recruited. I can give you a little idea of the way they are deserting. The 20th Michigan it seems marched from Morristown to this place and Charles Mench says he started on ahead and walked down the R.R. track six or seven miles, and in that distance he met no less than 15 deserters. They are coming in constantly, singly and in squads, while hundreds of Unionists in this state and from North Caroline, who have been kept under by the reign of terror, are organizing an army.

"It rained all this forenoon and is still cloudy and showery. I remember that 2 years ago today our little Nellie left us. But still she is ours. The Lord gave and the Lord has taken away, Blessed be the name of the Lord. What a train of sad thoughts this day brings to me and yet all is well, and I have great reason to say: Bless the Lord, O my soul. One year ago today I reached home, weary and wounded, from which wound I shall never fully recover.

"Friday P.M. It is a beautiful day, my Kitty's birthday. How I wish I could see you today. I have just finished a letter to Mr. Hollister. I will write not much today for I find the mail does not leave the regiment until Sunday night. I hear a brass band over in town playing 'Hail Columbia.' I have heard them playing a great deal today. Enlistment is going on rapidly. Arms have been sent for to put into the hands of men who have been ground down 2½ years. I calculate if they get a chance to use them, the fire will fly. All is quiet here. It is said that Gen. Wilcox is coming with 10,000 men and was this side of Cumberland Gap yesterday. I have not been into town only to church last Sunday. I have not been out of camp since we came here last Monday morning.

"Sat. Evening. I have no news to write. I have not been out of camp today. I made out a requisition for clothing. One of our men came up with us from Michigan about a week ago who has never been with us since we left Detroit. He went home, as I did, on a 4 day furlough and thought he would not return. I presume he was arrested and sent here. It is rumored today that our mail has been captured somewhere between Cumberland Gap and Morristown. I hope it is not so for I suppose there was at least one letter for me in it from you: besides I might have to wait another week for a letter. We have had no mail since last Sunday. I understand that Gen. Burnside has mustered some 10,000 new recruits since he took this place. The town is full of men eager to enlist, and the Office of the Provost Marshall is thronged continually by men waiting to take the oath. There is a prospect of staying here a length of time. Everything suits me except the inconvenience of mail and I think that will soon be remedied.

"Sunday P.M. I have not been to church today. There could only 4 from the company go. It is somewhat windy but pleasant. The rumor that our mail was captured is contradicted. I hope it is unfounded. I expect that some of our officers are going to Michigan in 2 or 3 days for recruits. If the Col. goes or some other trusty man, I will send you 40 dollars to be mailed as near home as possible. I think I have got this paper greasy and it is almost impossible to make a mark on it. I have enjoyed this day very well. I have been alone since 9 o'clock, Mr. Snow having gone to church. I have been reading Jeremiah, in which I have but one more chapter to read. I find that when we are in camp, I have more time than formerly to read. I wish we could get some late papers. We are almost starving for news. I would like to go to church with you in Marshall or Kalamazoo tonight. Is either or both ministers returned. The State Fair is passed and I suppose you have been in Kalamazoo. I feel rejoiced when I think of the prospect of soon getting home. None of us expect to have any more fighting to do. It is pleasant to lie still and see loyal citizens who heretofore have been kept down arming, scouring the country, and arresting and bringing in their old secesh neighbors, their former masters. Many of the natives through here are so ignorant that they really supposed the Yankees had horns.

"I wish I could say to you that I have received a letter from you, but I think I shall get one in a day or two and I am contented. Tell Frank he had better chop wood as fast as he can while the weather is good. Give my love to all our loyal friends. Goodbye Darling. Your affectionate husband: H. B. Potter

40

"What a multitude of blunders I have made, I am neither drunk nor crazy."

"Knoxville, Ky. Wednesday, October 7th, 1863
"My Dear Wife:
"I had a letter partly written to you and as I was fixing my tent and bunk last night, the tent fell and the letter was soiled and torn so I conclude to commence again. I have still time to write as the mail does not leave the regiment until tomorrow night. We get no mail yet. It is now 10 days since we rec'd any. About 9 o'clock night before last just after I had *got to bed*, someone raised the cry of 'mail.' I got up and hurried to Head-quarters in my drawers and bareheaded, *only to find* to I had been deceived as also were several others who went to get their company mails.

"Mr. Snow and myself went on Monday and cut down a tree and got over a quart of chestnuts each, the largest I ever saw. They are ripe and begin to fall. I wish I could give you some. I believe *you are fond of them.* Tell Frank I should like to have him gather chestnuts with me.

"I visited the city of Knoxville yesterday. I went at 9 and returned at 1 glad enough to get back. There is but very little there to sell as they have not had a chance to get goods, and they will not sell even what they have unless customers have the exact change. I succeeded in getting a package of envelopes for 25 cts., 12 steel pins for 20 cts., and a bottle of blue ink for 15 cts. Besides partly to make change and partly for my appetite, I bought some apples, some gingerbread, and a glass of cider. I had always supposed that Knoxville was a very small village in a desolate place among the hills. It is true the ground is roll-ing but I think it adds to the beauty of the site; and under Yankee hands, it would make a splendid town. As it is, there is considerable beauty, very many handsome dwellings and yards. The Presbyterian Church edifice is a splendid brick building. There are 2 large and handsome buildings on a hill to the west of town which I took to be seminaries or college buildings. Their

41

jail is a gloomy heap of stone. There is a large two story building fixed up and used for a prison for rebels. This is full above and below. The streets are a good width, well paved and kept clean and neat.

"There is a learned grizzly bear in town which I intended to see. Several of our company had seen him and said they were well paid for their money (25 cts.). He is 4½ ft. high and 11 ft. long and weights 1800 pounds. He is educated and performs many feats. He eats 50 pounds of beef per day. I made the effort to go in but could not *make change*. I went to the place again at noon and the showman had gone to dinner and would be back in about an hour. My pass only runs to one o'clock, besides I knew that others wanted to go to town in the afternoon so I concluded to let the bear go.

"I have spilled nearly all the ink I bought yesterday and find I have lost my pens. All right. The reason of my getting blue ink was because I could find but one place where they had black ink and as they had nothing else I wanted, we could not *make change*. They seem very partial to blue.

"It rained all forenoon and is still cloudy and dark. Many of the men are building log cabins with fireplaces. All is quiet here and everything goes off pleasantly. Oh that I should get a letter from home. I hope all my letters reach you, even if I do not hear from you very often. Nearly all our men are around the fire fighting their battles over. Many of them pass days and weeks, and perhaps months without reading anything unless it is an occasional novel. I never wanted to read as much as I do now. Each night I feel dissatisfied with what I have done and resolve to improve my time to better advantage next day. Today I have read 70 hymns and 5 chapters in Ezikial and intend to read several more. It is 14 months today since I enlisted and time flies faster than ever. One year ago tomorrow, I think, we went to Kalamazoo. I long to hear not only from you but from our affairs on Kalamazoo. I hope to have a letter from Mr. Hollister soon.

"Thur. morning. I have just finished my breakfast and have but little time to write. We move at 9. We are going to Greenville or near I suppose. The 1st and 2nd brigades went 2 or 3 days ago. I must stop now and make out the morning report. I have carried in my report and found that the mail had gone from the regiment. It does not leave town today. So I will discontinue writing.

"Afternoon. We are still at Knoxville. We left camp at 8, crossed the river, and came to the depot where we are now. I have concluded to write a little more and leave it with Mr. Hess, who is detached from our company and is at Division Headquarters here. He is not going with us. It has been a beautiful day. It is clear and scarcely a breath of air stirring. I must not forget to tell you that nearly all the Tennessee ladies chew tobacco and the majority of them smoke. Isn't that charming. Imagine a beauiful Belle with her face painted with tobacco juice. They make no secret of it anymore than the Gentlemen (?) do for in the presence of strangers and gentlemen they will take a chew and treat their lady friends.

"Well, Darling, I shall have to close for Mr. Snow is going to carry a letter to Mr. Hess and I want to send this by him. I know this is a very poor letter; hardly worth sending; but I will try and do better next time. I have been into a large yard and seen a multitude of wagons that the rebels left there. A Northerner would take it for a kind of museum. There are all sorts and sizes and in all conditions but good. Some had been captured from the Federals. One I noticed was marked U.S. and had C.S. over it. I am very well and expecting good news from you. Give my love to all our loyal friends. In fact, we will never have any other. I have bought today a military book embracing all the laws necessary in the Army and all forms and orders in use. It is just what I need and will be very useful to me and when I get home, will do very well to put into our library. It cost me one dollar. Goodbye Kitty. Your affectionate husband: H. B. Potter"

"Knoxville, Tenn. Friday, Oct. 9th, 1863

"My Dear Wife:

"You see I am still at Knoxville. We expected to have left last night and I sent a letter to Mr. Hess to mail for me as he will not go with us. He mailed it this morning. The Michigan 27th went last night but when I woke up this morning, I found our entire brigade was still here. About 8 this morning a regiment of Cavalry and regiment of mounted Infantry came down from town, passed us, and passed out of sight behind the depot buildings and hills and I do not know which way they went. Soon after General Burnside came down, which caused great excitement. Our brigade except the 17th were on three trains nearly ready to start. There was no cars for us. A nice passenger was attached to one of the trains for Burnside and his staff. The general went into the car followed by 3 Major Generals, 5 Brigadiers, and a whole retinue of inferior officers, nearly filling the car. When they were all comportably seated, the old hero came out, passed through the crowd of citizens and 17th soldiers, talked a few minutes with our Colonel, and then mounted the engine tender and seated himself on the tool box among the wood. A Captain condescended to ride with him. The train moved off amid almost deafening cheers. The General uncovered his head in acknowledgement, but put it on as soon as possible, and commenced passing wood to the firemen. If the troops could be justified in idolizing any leader, it would be General Burnside. He not only plans but he is not afraid to dirty his fingers, to say nothing about gloves, for it is seldom he wears any.

"It is now nearly sundown and our coffee is nearly ready so I will discontinue writing for tonight. We are waiting for a train and expect to go before morning. It has been a clear warm day.

"Monday noon. We are now, after passing through a variety of scenes, 92 miles from Knoxville and 12 miles above Greenville. We left Knoxville about 9 Saturday morning and went 70 miles, within 10 miles of Greenville, as far as they dared to run as the rebels held Greenville. We stopped at a little village which I

44

think was called Blue Springs. Here our men were in line of battle, and in front we could hear occasional shots of artillery but it was sundown and the firing soon ceased. We learned that our brigade had been skirmishing all day and was about 2 miles to the left. It was too late to join the brigade so we marched a mile and went into the woods until morning.

"On Sunday morning we were called up at 3½ o'clock, ate our breakfast, and was on the march before daylight. We joined the brigade and got into line of battle. On Saturday night the rebels had made a desperate effort and driven our skirmishers back over the brow of a hill, on the side of which we were lying. All was still until 8 o'clock when it was determined to feel the enemy, and our skirmishers advanced but could find *nothing*. That was just as I expected. A large force of Cavalry then went thundering by in pursuit and we followed. A small force of Cavalry had been sent around to get in their rear and hold them in check. After passing Greenville we heard they were fighting about 4 miles, and we hurried on, but soon heard they *were 8* miles ahead; and kept just about 7 or 8 miles ahead of us all afternoon. We chased them 20 miles, which I think was a big days work for Sunday. They commenced skirmishing soon after passing Greenville and continued it for 15 miles when the (our) Cavalry stopped 3 miles ahead of here where they now are. We are to move at 2 o'clock, which will be in a few minutes, and I shall have to get ready.

"Well, we were called to attention and got our things on when the order was countermanded. Then there was a rush made for rails to burn tonight and in five minutes 100 rods of fence *was* moving into the camps. The Cavalry is coming back, each having a bundle of oats or hay behind him. The first obsticle we met in the pursuit was a *rail fence* which the sagacious rebels had built across the road but it was demolished in less time than it was built. Before night we passed several wagons which they had to abandon, one had been loaded with beef but was then empty. An ammunition wagon with several boxes of artillery ammunition fell into our hands. One canister cartridge was

45

opened here a short time ago. It consisted of a tin can $3\frac{1}{2}$ inches in diameter and 6 inches long filled with iron balls (60) about as large as this or perhaps larger. Attached to one end of this is a pound of powder in a bag. So you see, they can load very quick. Several rebels are being buried here. Five of our men were killed in the skirmish along the road and several surrounded. There were 3 thousand went this road and they might have been baged if the officer who was sent around to their rear had done his duty. He headed them, had a skirmish, and let them pass. We understand that Burnside has put him under arrest.

"Thursday P.M. We have just arrived at Morristown 42 miles from where I last wrote. We have marched all the way. We started on Tuesday morning and marched 15 miles, and then went a mile from the road to the R.R. expecting to take the cars but found we could not, we have so few cars in our possession and they are very busy carrying supplies. The officers had sent their horses ahead, expecting to go on the railroad, and they have had to foot it now for two days. (Poor Souls) We started at sunrise yesterday and marched 12 miles. There we got a big mail and, Of Joy! I received yours of September 18th and was more than happy to get it and hear that you were doing so well.

"I think those samples you sent are nice. I should like to see Nettie in her cloak. The stamps are all right. I now have 13. I am pleased with Frank's letter. How does he act now. If I do not get time to answer it this time (and I fear I shall not), will you tell him I rec'd his and think it is a good letter. Tell him I am marching every day and do not have much time to write.

"We somewhat expected to ride from where we lay last night but could not. We started this morning before sunrise and marched 15 miles. It is possible we may ride from here, but I do not expect it. It is $4\frac{1}{2}$ o'clock and if we march tomorrow, we shall go early. We are going back to Knoxville. I think it is possible we may go from here on the cars for when we came in, our brigade all formed in line parallel with the R.R. and stacked arms about 12 rods from the track. It is cloudy and decidedly cool. I must go now and pitch my tent, and get something for feathers, and see about my supper.

"Saturday morning. At Knoxville again and *all is well*. We got a large mail last night and I rec'd your long precious letter of the 28th. together with Nettie's. I believe I have a little witch at home. I cannot tell you how much good your letters do me. They make me decidedly happy. I rec'd by the same mail the package of 3 papers you mentioned, also a package containing a Rural and Northwestern which I suppose you sent. I am glad to get them and greatly obliged. I also rec'd a letter from Sarah and James, which I shall try to answer in time for the next mail which leaves the reg't tomorrow night. I rec'd last night a note from Mrs. Alger, whose husband we left with 6 others sick at Crabb Orchard. When we left there, he wished me to write to his wife (although I think he was abundantly able to write for himself). I accordingly wrote a hasty letter to her while on the march over the mountains and now she wants all the particulars *immediately*. He asked me to read a letter to him just before we left as his eyes were so weak. In that she told him she thought his last letter was unkind and said she could not write again until he sent some money to pay postage. Darling, the more I see of the world the more I am convinced that not more than one couple in twenty live as agreeable as you and I. I must also write immediately to Sergeant Jackson, one of the sick at Crabb Orchard, and forward his mail to him. So you see I have got something to do.

"The call to 'strike tents' was sounded yesterday morning before we had cooked our breakfast. We packed our things ready to start and then cooked our breakfast but just as we were ready to eat, the 'fall in' call was sounded and Mr. Snow carried our coffee in our pail and meat in the frying pan and we ate after we got on the cars. There was a drizzling rain nearly all the way through which continued until near night. There were 2 regiments on the train and we run very slowly on account of heavy grades, stopping a number of times and backing up to get more motion. We reached Knoxville about 1 o'clock and marched 1 mile east of this town and are in camp in the woods again. The Colonel told us to take plenty of ground and lay out our camp in good style for he did not know how long we might stay here. It is said by some that we are to go to the other side of the river Monday but I do not care which side of the river we stay.

"It is a beautiful day. I got 2 kinds of flower seed last Sunday while chasing the rebels, some of which I will send in this if I do not forget it. The smallest seeds were on a small stalk. Probably you will know what they are as soon as you see them. The large ones grew on a tree about 10 feet high with a large top. It was full of buds.

"Sunday morning. It is a pleasant morning and I wish I could talk with you instead of writing. I washed my clothes yesterday P.M. The skirmish picture is not taken from life, but it is as lifelike as though it has been taken on the skirmish line. It was taken at Nicholasville, or at our camp, rather, near there, in a car. A number of skirmish pictures had been taken and 3 of our men in Co. 1 wanted to get theirs taken and after hesitating some time, I concluded to go in with them. They cost one dollar. We got them for 2 shillings less than his usual price by taking four. He could not take but 3 in a group. He carried in bushes and stumps. There is a stump in front of Mr. Snow which does not show in the picture.

"I have just rec'd and read your letter of Oct. 8th which brings such sad news of Uncles sickness. I fear it will go hard with him, he is so old and has always been so strong and hearty. I do not apprehend any trouble with the French. No doubt they will bluster to scare us if they can. I should like to be there to pare apples again this fall. I am glad you rec'd all the money and as soon as I find that you get letters from here, I shall send more. I rejoice that our debts are being paid. At least when I get out of the service, we shall have enough to pay the last cent and have some left besides clearing our home. Darling, while you have so much to do, please write short letters. I rejoice to get long ones but I want to hear from you often and if you just say how you all are, I will be content.

"It has commenced raining and I fear I cannot write much today. We are not intended to reinforce Rosecrans. It is Burnsides business to hold East Tennessee and he will hold it effectually. I am glad to hear so good a report from our home. I did not expect the fruit trees would bear any this season. I trust if they bear next summer, we shall receive the benefit. I am glad Mr. Hollister's folks are going to be our neighbors still. I am very sorry you could not visit Nellie's grave. If I should ever get a furlough, I will go by way of Alton. How much I would have enjoyed the Fair with you. I am very glad to hear that Ma is better. I think little Emma will soon be big Emma if she goes ahead as she has done. How I wish I could see her, and all the rest of you, especially as you are having so much sickness. I am *very thankful* you have got along so well. I am *very* glad you have got a good shawl and bonnet. I really hope you will want for nothing as long as you have money. You must not pass the winter without getting a dress.

"I am Acting Orderly. I cannot be appointed until the former Orderly, who has been promoted to 2nd Lt., receives his commission. If it comes before we are paid, my promotion will date back to Sept. 14; if not, I shall only get 17 dollars for this present time. I have rec'd no letter from Mr. Wood and feel disappointed. Darling, I fear you will overdo; be very careful, won't you. I cannot tell how James Reese acts now. I only see him occasionally for a minute or two. I will ask Harvey Seymour about him the first opportunity. I am not aware that Burnside was ordered to reinforce Rosecrans any more than to hold this road. Rosecrans is all right. 14 miles march was as much as any of us could stand the day you mentioned. When I have endured all that I ought, I fall out. My marching has not hurt me. I feel as *fresh and young* as I *ever did*. How I would like to know how Uncle is. I shall anxiously wait for another letter. Ask Sarah and James to bear with me until the next mail. I have so much to do and the mail leaves soon now. I will try and write to them tomorrow. Tell Frank I will try and write him a long letter the next time I write to you.

49

"After mailing my letter on the 17th of Sept., I had no opportunity to mail another until the 24 which partially accounts for your not hearing from me in a long time. It has now been 8 days since I could mail one. I will answer the letter I got this morning in my next. I am *very* well and *fat*. It still rains. I hope soon to hear better news from home. All is well. Give my love to all our friends. Tell James I am glad to see his letter and will try and answer it tomorrow. I wish you would keep me informed of Frank's conduct. Goodby Dear. Your affectionate hubby: H. B. Potter"

"Loudon, Tennessee
"My Dear Wife:
    "It is a cold rainy day but I must, if possible, write a letter. We slept without a tent last night but just at daylight, it began to rain and we pitched out tent in a hurry. I mailed a letter to you last Sunday. I wrote to Sarah and James on Monday and Monday evening and Tuesday evening I wrote a few lines to you and enclosed 40 dollars which I sent, together with James and Sarahs letter, by a man of Co. D who was going to Detroit. In that I told you it was said we were going 40 miles, 10 miles beyond Loudon, to guard a bridge which was being built. The said bridge is, or was, here and is *not* being rebuilt. It was a very long and high bridge.
    "We left camp at 7 o'clock Tuesday morning and marched 16 miles. It was a nice day but the roads were very bad in places and we marched considerable through the fields and woods. We stopped 2 hours for dinner and heard cannonading in the distance. We camped in an open field and started again Wednesday morning, just at daylight, and marched until noon, 11 miles. About 9 it began to rain and continued nearly all day. It rained about an hour quite hard and when it got very muddy and slippery, we got onto the R.R. track and walked about 4 miles. About a mile before we stopped, we left the track. We stopped in the woods, and rumor says we had been ordered to Kingston and had taken the wrong road. In a short time, the Colonel told

us to pitch our tents and make ourselves as comfortable as we could until next morning.

"We remained there until afternoon yesterday and then came to this place 4 miles. We crossed the river in a pontoon bridge. This is quite a town, lying on the south side of the river which is here a large and beautiful river. I suppose we are to go to Kingston after the rain is over. Kingston is 16 miles north of west of here. The troops through here are building winter quarters but I think they are only for those guarding the road.

"Afternoon. This is one of our most disagreeable days, a cold rainy day. Darling, you must not expect to hear from me for quite a while as regularly as formerly. There are times when I cannot send a letter out for a week and there may be times when I cannot send as often as that. Besides it is *very* inconvenient to write while on the march; but I shall endeavor to write as often as there is a chance to mail a letter, if I can only write a few lines. But Kitty, of one thing you may be assured: I am *always* well and doing well.

"It seems hard that I could not get a furlough but when the war is over and I get home to stay, we shall be glad I did not and I know all will be for the best. I do not apprehend any trouble from the French. No doubt much will be said to frighten us at this critical time, this turning of the disease.

"I am glad Mr. Hemenway is stationed at Kalamazoo and believe we shall hear him preach before this year expires. What a wretch that Clay is. Then it seems that he was a widower. Perhaps he has *got* a score of wives. It will be well for him to keep a respectful distance from me. Is it not strange that Ruby is so unfortunate? I should think she would go crazy. I am glad Thomas is sending her money. He will not permit her to suffer so long as he has a dollar. I believe him to be a noble fellow. I am glad Ruby will have nothing to do with Clay. She is indeed placed in trying circumstances. I am very sorry for her and wish I could do something for her, and perhaps I can in time. I am glad you went to the County Fair and took Frank. I am glad you give something to the children besides quinine. I have a horror of that stuff. It is the principle medicine in the Army for *everything* and many a poor fellow has been almost used up by it.

"Sunday. How many Sabbaths must I spend in the Army. This day is passing very agreeably. I have written to Frank and now must write to Kitty. I am very well. It is a pleasant, but cool day. When we came here, the rebels were only 5 or 6 miles from here about 15,000 strong. Skirmishing has been going on, more or less, for some days. Our men had been at one time driven back to this town but in turn, drove the rebels back and held them there. Yesterday afternoon the hosts of Cavalry and some artillary began to move towards the front and soon we heard cannonading. About 3 o'clock, the Infantry were ordered to strike tents. We fell in on the 'Color Line' and stacked arms, got everything ready in haste, and waited for the 'Assembly' to sound but night came and everything remained quiet. So we pitched our tents again and lay down, expecting to be called up before morning; but morning found us here and brought news that the rebels had fled and could not be found. I think we shall now proceed to Kingston but I hope we will not have to start today, though I just heard we had got marching orders. I wish quietly to enjoy this day in camp.

"Darling, I wish you to keep me informed in regard to Frank's conduct and I will write to him accordingly. I am anxious to hear from Uncle. How I would like to be at home to help do his Fall work. Is James able to do much? I dreamed last night of being there, and have several nights of late. The prospect is that I shall soon be there to stay and the thought is *cheering*. How rapidly the time flies. It is over 10 months since I left you. It is clearing off today and looks some like Indian Summer. We draw soft bread again here. We use hard bread only on the march as we can carry 3 days of rations about as easy as one of soft bread, but potatoes are unknown to us. We have drawn them but 2 or 3 times sinces we left Newport News. I fear I shall want them 3 times a day when I get home and

52

perhaps some between meals. I hope Mrs. Garder will watch the things in our shop and see that they are not injured by being wet for I fear the roof leaks.

"If I do not forget it, I will send some more of the flower seeds in this like those I sent in my last. I mean to save some Persimmon seed, which grows here abundantly wild. The trees sometimes grow to the height of 30 feet. The fruit is about the size of crab apples and when ripe, is second only to peaches. I do not know as it will mature or even grow in a Northern climate, but it will not cost much to try it. I want to reap all the benefit I can from my exile. I feel some anxiety about the money I sent last. If it should not reach you, it would be quite a loss. I thought it the best and safest thing I could do with it. We rec'd mail last night. I hope the next will bring good news from home. I cannot learn whether the mail leaves the regiment or not but to make sure, I will put this in the bag. There is no signs of moving yet and I think we will lay here until morning. It is now about 3 o'clock. I hope you have been to church today. I have not much church privileges. Our Chaplain was left in Kentucky. *Poor soul.*

"Now Darling, do not be anxious about me if you do not get letters very often. I presume this will not leave Knoxville until Wednesday. Take good care of yourself and I shall do the same. Give my love to our friends. All is *well.* Goodbye Darling. Kiss the *little* girls for me. May the Lord bless and keep you is prayer of your affectionate husband: H. B. Potter"

"Loudon, Tenn. Tuesday October 27, 1863
"My Dear Wife:
"Here I am yet on the ground where I wrote last. I mailed a letter to you day before yesterday. We were then expecting hourly to move but have got over it now. I have just finished a letter to Mrs. Clay. It is cloudy and showery today. Yesterday was a beautiful day. We are lying here quietly doing nothing. The position of the rebels is about the same as when we came here. The report that they had gone was without foundation. They seem to be foraging and keep up a bold front to intimidate

us. Burnside is very busy preparing to spring a trap on them. It is said that skirmishing is going on daily. Now and then a heavy Cavalry force is sent out to threaten them and then retire as though we wanted to attack them but dare not. While behind the curtain, operations are active which probably only Rosecrans and Burnside understand. Burnside says he is going to have this road to Chattanooga within 3 weeks.

"Our trains are sent out all through the County for forage. They go 20 or 30 together, each team being guarded by 2 or 3 men. I sent 4 men today for forage guards, 3 of them to be gone 2 days and the others one day. I was up this morning at 4 o'clock (as I had to get the forage guards off at 5), I built a fire just outside my tent, and went to reading by firelight and finished the Bible. I have read the Old and New Testaments and Hymn Book through and have turned back to the beginning again resolved, if possible, to have my mind on what I read better than before. I find it very difficult to confine myself to what I am reading while surrounded by so much noise and confusion; but I intend this time to understand what I read, if I have to read each chapter over a number of times. The love of reading grows on me. I cannot read enough and feel sorry when night comes and am glad to hail the morning. How gladly would I employ some of my spare time in helping you take care of the children, or *wipe the dishes* for you, or sweep. I presume you have but little time to read. You shall have more leisure time when I get home.

"Friday P.M. Another change and not a disagreeable one; on Wednesday morning all our force was on the move at daybreak, and re-crossed the river, and took up the bridge. Speculation began to run high. Some thought the rebels were too strong for us and we were going to retreat; some thought the rebels had changed their position and we must necessarily move; some thought a force of Rosecrans was driving them toward us and we were only going to cross the river and wait for them. Others thought we had got to fall back to Kentucky and give this place up.

"Saturday. I was obliged to stop writing yesterday on account of the rain. It rained nearly all day and all night last night. It is cloudy and dark today. After crossing the river we marched about a mile and stopped by the side of the road until afternoon for the wagon train and Cavalry to pass. As the 8th Michigan Cavalry passed, I am quite sure I saw (I do not remember the name) the man that was clerk in Phelps and Smith's store. He looked very smiling but did not see me, I think. I did not see him until he had passed and there was such a crowd I could not have got to him.

"We marched in the P.M. 6 miles towards Knoxville and camped until afternoon next day when we started again, and marched 1½ miles to this place. We were (our brigade) formed in line and stacked arms. All the commissioned officers of the brigade then got together for a council, this we had never seen before. When they returned to their commands, we were informed that *we would probably stay here all winter!!!* Well we were a happy set for we have seen a great deal of active service since the frost got out of the ground last spring, and perhaps we can do as much good lying here and holding the rebels to it as we could do by marching all the time and fighting some.

"We have got a beautiful situation, on a hill, in the woods with the railroad in front, and river in the rear about ½ mile I think. We were ordered to leave the large trees in camp and cut the small ones. We only had time before dark to pitch our tents and in the evening, myself and three others went ¾ of a mile to Lenoir Station to get some brick for a fireplace from an old brick building that has been burned there. There were perhaps 400,000 bricks but they were going like the dew before the sun. We tied them up in a half tent and slung them on a pole and carried them on our shoulders. We got back to camp about 9 o'clock but thought, to make sure of them, we would go again knowing that men would be carrying them off all night. Some were bringing them up on a hand car, putting on about a thousand at a load, and piling them up by the track near their regiments. We brought 96, which will make a nice fireplace, and

55

we will build the chimney of wood and mortar. Yesterday morning we heard that the brick were nearly all gone, and a guard was placed over what remained, and not even a piece could be got; those that had been run off on the cars was also guarded. They want them to build a bakery. I conclude I am fortunate. A great many got them that night and will keep them.

"Yesterday forenoon we cut the logs for our house and brought them up. It was raining nearly all day. In the afternoon it rained so that we could not work and I tried to write but it was too damp in the tent. It is now clearing off. We shall live four in a house. I am entitled to a house alone but do not wish it. Mr. Snow, Orton, and Dunning, a single man, are with me. There is a large creek at the foot of the hill and a spring large enough to turn a small mill. By referring to the map, you can see where we are. We are 7 miles east of Loudon (where the R.R. crossed the river). Perhaps the town is not laid down between the R.R. and the river. I have been very busy since we came here. I can write but a few lines without stopping to do something. We have just mustered for pay. We muster every 2 months and yet how very often they seem to come. We intend to build our house Monday. There is a large quantity of clothing at Knoxville for us. It will soon be brought down. *How glad I am* that we have not got to fall back to Kentucky.

"Sunday. It is a lovely day but all bustle here. At least 4/5ths of the men in camp are at work on their houses. Some whose conscience twings a little try to believe it is necessary. We shall commence ours before daylight tomorrow morning and before this reaches you, we shall be settled in our new house. We received a small mail last night, 3 letters for our company. Those officers have to go to Michigan to recruit. It is a week today since I had a letter. I am very anxious to hear from you; to know not only how you get along, but to hear how Uncle is. Some 700 rebels crossed the river not many miles below here last Friday and 400 were captured before they could re-cross. I think we shall accomplish much by lying here and holding

East Tennessee, perhaps more than by marching all winter. I suppose the draft has been enforced in Michigan.

"I should be very happy to go to church with you today. But I hope soon to have that privilege. I am often astonished when I think how time flies. It seems that Emma is almost 7 months old. It seems hardly possible. Does Nettie seem inclined to talk any yet? Now Darling, you may be sure I shall have a good time. I sent 40 dollars to you on the 19th. Goodby Kitty. Love to all friends. Your affectionate husband: H. B. Potter"

"Lenoir Station, Tenn. Thur. November 5th, 1863
"My Dear Wife:
"It is a rainy day but in my new house it is not so damp as to prevent my writing. I mailed a letter to you last Sunday and now wish to mail this today. Mr. Orton and I are alone today, the others being on picket. Mr. Orton is our Commissary Sergeant. Two of our company, which we left in hospital in Baltimore, have just come up.

"We have just got our house finished. I will send you a plan of it. We only got it nicely started on Monday. I was out carrying stone for the fireplace an hour before daylight. I got enough to build it up to the crossbar, which is a flat bar of iron. We also have an iron bar to hang kettles on. I had brick enough to finish the whole chimney. I built the chimney and the others put up the house, and chinked it, and I mudded it. I built the best looking fireplace and chimney in the regiment, and some thought I was putting on style, but it *did* smoke; and this forenoon I took it down to the crossbar and built it over, and now it draws good. I got it done just as it began to rain. Our house stands the end of the street. It is 7 by 9 feet. The door in the front end and the fireplace on the other side. On the opposite side we have a table about 8 inches wide fixed up to the logs, and on the back end two bunks. Mr. Snow and I sleep on the lower one. We have nails and pins to hang our guns, equipments, clothing, cups, and so forth on. Our fireplace is as large as is usually made for a dining room or parlor. In short, we are nicely situated. We have each a stool and yesterday I found a nice pile of feathers where some geese had been picked and have got them for a pillow.

"I received last Sunday your precious letter of Oct. 18th. and was, as usual, *very* glad to hear from you and to hear that you are doing so well. I had hoped to hear a better report in regard to Uncle but am glad it was no worse. How I wish I was there. I suppose if that 40 dollars goes safe, you have got it before this time. Do you miss me at home? I miss my home and family and friends. But still it is only for a season. I too realize the preciousness of the privilege of prayer and daily commit my family and friends and all our interest into the care of Him who careth for us. Darling, this is why I am so content. I dare not disbelieve Him, and it cheers my heart to get such letters from you. Let us live that we may turn all our trials into *real* blessings. This is our privilege, and I am resolved to do it. You have suffered much since I enlisted, but I do not know of an enlisted man that has had as easy times as I have. Everything seems to be in my favor. Ninety-five days absent from the regiment last Fall during the hardest marching of the regiment and worst weather then. Then five months that all I had to do was to draw rations, and now I do not have that to do; and at this moment Mr. Orton is off in the rain drawing fresh beef. I never have drilled more than 8 days at 2 hours a day, and have had nothing to do with guard or picket duty but 7 days. I have acted 3 times as Sergeant of the Picket and 5 times Sergeant of the Guard. And now that is all done away with. And now I have a good house and everything comfortable.

"Friday morning. You see I did not finish my letter yesterday and I must write fast this morning for we have general inspection at 11, and I have got to put my gun and equipment in shining order. It is a beautiful morn but it rained nearly all night.

"Wallandingham's defeat was partly owing to the soldiers having the privilege of voting. They voted in our return trip from the Greenville expedition. So you see, as we went out, we drove Southern traitors and on our return defeated *Northern traitors*. This shows what the Army is composed of.

"I am afraid, Kitty, you are doing too much work. I wish you would hire a girl and pay her out of our money. Do be *careful*. I am very glad you got those apples. I should like to eat them with you but never mind, the time will soon come that I shall be with you. Darling, do not give up doctoring with Price until every vestige of disease is removed. Do not spare money until you *are perfectly* well. I am very glad to hear that you *can* work like everything, but I beg you be very careful. I know you have been *very* bad off, and now do be careful.

"I think this is the time for speculators to enlist. There is some difference between six hundred dollars and 40 for a bounty. But I shall feel as well as those that made rich out of our country's troubles. When it is decided who goes, I wish you would inform me. I think we have enough men in the field now, and the President will probably only keep the number good unless it should be necessary to have another campaign. If so, I hope he will send an overwhelming force. I hope you have got that Sept. letter before this time. Is that the only one you have lost? Burnside was very warmly welcomed at Knoxville and in fact, in nearly all East Tennessee. But there are some localities where secession predominates. Was not my letter of Sept. 15th finished at Knoxville. If so, I only wrote one before that and the one of Oct. 1st, which I think was dated Sept. 25th. I have received at least five of the seven papers you mention. If now and then one is lost, never mind; let them come.

"Afternoon. Well I had to stop for inspection and then had a long requisition for clothing, equipment, etc. to make out. Destruction to Charleston, I think, is inevitable. The rebels, it seems, are determined to burn it if compelled to give it up. Fredericksburg — like our pickets stand along one bank of the river and the rebel pickets on the other and often talk with each other. Some of them told our men last night that they are not *mad* at us and it was too bad that we were fighting each other.

59

"I am surprised to such news from, or about games. It does not seem possible. I shall wait with some anxiety to hear the sequel to this. I shall not object to your going in the Spring. I believe I shall soon follow you if I am not there to go with you. Oh I hope I can be there in the Spring in time to make garden. The convalescents that came up from Baltimore say they heard several rebel officers, who were taken prisoners at Gettysburg, say that as soon as our Congress convenes, they intend to offer to settle this up. They said all they expected to do was to hold out until that time.

"Darling, let me know in your next just what your prospect is for wood. I should think some of the neighbors could get you some wood for the money. Kitty, you say you did not mean to write me about your trouble for wood. Do you wish me to keep my troubles from you? In regard to Dr. Comstock and Lady leaving the M. E. Church; I should say good riddance to driftwood. 'For the days will come in which they will not endure sound doctrine.' I admire the dress and aprons for the girls. How strange it seems to write about our girls. Little Emma is 7 months old today it seems. Well, well, I dream almost nightly about being at home. Tell Frank to do the best he can for wood. Give my love to our friends. Goodby precious. Your affectionate husband: H. B. Potter

"My health is improving."

DIARY

"FRIDAY, NOV. 6

GENERAL INSPECTION BY THE INSPECTOR GENERAL. MADE A REQUISITION FOR CLOTHING AND EQUIPMENT. PLEASANT DAY. ALL IS WELL."

"SATURDAY, NOV. 7

CALLED UP LAST NIGHT AT ELEVEN O'CLOCK AND ORDERED TO PACK UP OUR THINGS, TAKE OUR TENTS OFF FROM OUR HOUSES, AND BE READY TO MOVE. GOT SOME BREAKFAST AND WENT TO THE R.R. AND GOT ON THE TRAIN AND LEFT AT 3 FOR KNOXVILLE. COLD, FROSTY MORNING. ARRIVED AT KNOXVILLE AT 8½ O'CLOCK AND LAY AT THE DEPOT UNTIL 3 P.M. THEN MOVED BACK A LITTLE AND CAMPED FOR THE NIGHT. RECEIVED A LETTER FROM KITTY. VERY PLEASANT. MAILED A LETTER TO KITTY."

"SUNDAY, NOV. 8

LYING AT KNOXVILLE EXPECTING TO RETURN TO OUR WINTER QUARTERS. CLOUDY AND COLD. DOES NOT SEEM MUCH LIKE THE SABBATH. 'OH FOR A CLOSER WALK WITH GOD.' "

"MONDAY, NOV. 9

CLOUDY AND COLD WITH FLURRIES OF SNOW. TOOK THE CARS AT 1 O'CLOCK P.M. FOR LENOIR, OUR WINTER QUARTERS. ARRIVED AT 5½ O'CLOCK P.M., COLD ENOUGH. FOUND FIRES IN OUR HOUSES."

"TUESDAY, NOV. 10

SOMEWHAT UNWELL WITH A COLD. ISSUED SOME CLOTHING TO THE COMPANY AND DREW A PAIR OF SOCKS AND A PAIR OF DRAWERS. PLEASANT. 'REST FOR MY SOUL I LONG TO FIND.' "

"WEDNESDAY, NOV. 11

PLEASANT DAY. SENT OUT A FORAGE PARTY AT DAY-
BREAK, AND THE REGT. FELL IN AND STACKED ARMS
AT THE SAME TIME. READY TO MOVE AT A MOMENT'S
NOTICE SHOULD THE REBELS MAKE A DEMONSTRA-
TION."

"THURSDAY, NOV. 12

STACKED ARMS AGAIN AT DAYLIGHT. ALL QUIET
THROUGH THE DAY. MAILED A LETTER TO KITTY."

"FRIDAY, NOV. 13

RECEIVED INTELLIGENCE OF THE DEATH OF
THOMAS. THIS TAKES MY LAST BROTHER, AND YET
I AM SPARED AND STAND STRONG TRUSTING IN THE
GOD OF BATTLES. I MUST TRY AND DO THE WORK
OF THREE."

"SATURDAY, NOV. 14

MARCHED IN P.M. 5 MILES BELOW LOUDON WHERE
THE REBELS WERE CROSSING. FIGHTING GOING ON.
RAINED DURING THE NIGHT."

"SUNDAY, NOV. 15

STARTED BACK ½ HOUR BEFORE DAYLIGHT AND
MARCHED TO LENOIR STATION WITHIN ¼ MILE
OF OUR WINTER QUARTERS. MADE COFFEE. FELL IN
AT 2 P.M. AND MARCHED ½ MILE AND FORMED IN
LINE OF BATTLE. SAW THE REBEL SKIRMISHERS
ADVANCING. LAY ON OUR ARMS."

"MONDAY, NOV. 16

COMMENCED RETREATING FOR KNOXVILLE AT 2
O'CLOCK A.M. WENT WHERE WE GOT COFFEE YESTER-
DAY AND LAY UNTIL DAYLIGHT. DESTROYED OUR
WAGON TRAINS, AMMUNITION, SUPPLIES, AND
EVERYTHING WE COULD NOT MOVE. OUR REGIMENT

COVERED THE RETREAT. THE REBELS ATTACK US IN THE REAR. WE MAKE 2 STANDS AND FIGHT THEM ALONE. WHEN WE MAKE OUR THIRD STAND, THE MICH. 20 HELP US. HERE I GOT WOUNDED IN THE LEFT CHEEK. RIDE 18 MILES TO K IN AMBULANCE."

"TUESDAY, NOV. 17
FIND MYSELF IN THE ASYLUM HOSPITAL AT KNOXVILLE. FEEL RATHER SLIM."

"WEDNESDAY, NOV. 18
BATTLE STILL RAGING. 600 PRISONERS BROUGHT IN. LORD GIVE US SUCCESS. WROTE TO KITTY BUT CANNOT SEND IT. THE LORD BE PRAISED THAT I AM SO WELL OFF."

"THURSDAY, NOV. 19
THE REBELS HAVE SURROUNDED US BUT WE FEEL CONFIDENCE IN HOLDING THE PLACE. THEY HAVE ONE BAT. IN POSITION. NOT VERY GOOD."

"FRIDAY, NOV. 20
I AM MOVED FROM THE FLOOR IN A COLD DARK HALL TO A BED IN A WARM ROOM. SKIRMISHING ALL DAY. OUR REGIMENT ORDERED TO BURN SOME BUILDINGS IN THE EVEN. BEYOND OUR SKIRMISHERS, WHICH THEY ACCOMPLISHED, BUT IN RETIRING WERE SHELLED BY THE ENEMY AND A 2nd LIEUTENANT KILLED WHEN OUR BATTERIES OPENED ON THE REBELS. RAINED ALL NIGHT."

"SATURDAY, NOV. 21
RAINY ALL DAY. LIGHT SKIRMISHING. I AM QUITE COMFORTABLE. 'GREAT PEACE HAVE THEY THAT LOVE THY LAW, AND NOTHING SHALL OFFEND THEM.' "

"SUNDAY, NOV. 22

BEAUTIFUL DAY BUT SEEMS VERY LITTLE LIKE THE SABBATH. OUR CHAPLAIN HAS COME UP. WHAT WILL HE DO? LORD SAVE HIM AND US. STILL SKIRMISHING."

"MONDAY, NOV. 23

BEAUTIFUL DAY. MY EYES ARE SO WEAK THAT I CAN READ BUT LITTLE. VERY LIGHT SKIRMISHING."

> Sgt. Homer B. Potter died shortly after this final entry was made in his diary. He was buried at the military cemetery near Knoxville, Tennessee.
> The illustration at the head of this chapter was made at the burial site and is a detailed illustration of the actual monument that marks his last resting place.

Chapter IV

ARMY OF THE GRAND TRAVERSE

On February 14, 1895, in a small room over the James Scofield blacksmith shop, located in the 400 block between East State street and East Front street in Traverse City, Michigan, the Hannah Rifles was organized.

The organization, first military group in the Grand Traverse Region of Michigan, was named in honor of the leading citizen of Traverse City, Perry Hannah, lumber baron and one of the founders of the village of Traverse City.

The organizational meeting on Valentine's Day was not, however, the first attempt to bring into being a military unit in Traverse City.

On June 5, 1894, a meeting was called in the law offices of Manley C. Dodge and George Covell in the City Opera House to discuss the possibility of organizing a permanent military group whose aim was to become a part of the National Guard. The meeting accomplished very little, although a number of the men who attended, including Captain J. V. McIntosh, later became affiliated with the Hannah Rifles.

On the following December 5, 1894, a second attempt was made to establish a military company or organization. At this meeting a civil organization was created with Claire Curtis as president; Claude Palamatier, secretary; and Theron Densmore, treasurer.

The next meeting of the group was held December 13, 1894, and three men, J. W. Hannen, P. C. Gilbert, and Fred D. Curtis were appointed to draft by-laws and a constitution.

Then, on December 27, 1894, what was pronounced as a permanent military organization was completed and officers were named by the members.

67

The new officers were: T. L. Densmore, captain; Fred D. Curtis, 1st lieutenant; H. K. Knapp, 2nd lieutenant; O. E. Thomas, quartermaster; Claire Curtis, president; Claude Palmatier, secretary; and P. C. Gilbert, treasurer.

The new company was named the "Traverse City Light Guards." Following this initial organization there was a falling off of interest, and the inexperience of Captain Densmore caused the company to all but fall apart.

Then new life was instilled on February 14, 1895, when the "Traverse City Light Guards" was completely disbanded and a new company formed. It was named in honor of Perry Hannah and became the Hannah Rifles. As such, it marched 110 strong to fight in the Spanish-American War.

New officers to serve the Hannah Rifles were: Captain, J. V. McIntosh; 1st Lieutenant, Fred D. Curtis; 2nd Lieutenant, Joseph Klaasen; President, J. W. Hannen; Secretary, Claude Palmatier; and Treasurer, Claire Curtis.

Following the reorganization of the company, the men met for first drill on February 18, 1895. With the entire company in formation, President J. W. Hannen read a communication from Perry Hannah, in whose honor the company was named.

"Dear Sir:

"I notice that the young men who are members of the new military company just organized in Traverse City, have done me the honor of naming the company with my name.

"I am pleased with the compliment and I am more than grateful with their loyalty to Traverse City. Any move that insures to the good of our town gives me great pleasure. Enclosed I hand you my check for one hundred ($100) to help pay expenses.

"Yours very truly,
Perry Hannah"

A public meeting was scheduled for March 6th and it was a rouser, indeed. The City Opera House was packed and there was a program of song and patriotic speeches. Hannah was the honored guest on the occasion.

During the program Miss Capitola Vader and Miss Josephine Wilhelm sang their very best soprano, as did Miss Gertrude Sprague and Miss Alma Despres. Judge Lorin Roberts delivered a stirring speech in behalf of the citizens of the community and P. C. Gilbert responded with a speech on behalf of the men of the company.

A long resolution was presented and inscribed on the records of the company in which Perry Hannah was thanked several times. In addition to the presentation of resolutions, Perry Hannah was presented with an embossed certificate which made him a member of the company as long as he lived.

There was a lack of drill equipment for the new company and McPherson Post, G.A.R., loaned the members rifles with which to work once each week.

The matter of proper uniforms for the Hannah Rifles was the next business to come before the group. A public subscription campaign was launched and it was only a few days until there was six hundred dollars available, of which Perry Hannah again contributed one hundred.

The weekly drills took place for nearly three years in Library Hall, another and less common name for the Ladies' Library on East Front Street. The participation of the members in parades and on festive occasions was the pride of the community.

The first non-commissioned officers in the Hannah Rifles were: 1st Sergeant Claire Curtis, 2nd Sergeant J. A. McDonald, 3rd Sergeant H. I. Knapp, 4th Sergeant Charles M. Beers, 5th Sergeant P. C. Gilbert, and Quartermaster Oscar E. Thomas.

On May 5, 1895, the new uniforms, which the public had contributed money to purchase, were revealed to the public for the first time. It was during the annual Memorial Day Parade and they were Union Army uniforms of the Civil War.

One of the spectacular events in the life of the Hannah Rifles was a banquet and reception given in Library Hall on June 19, 1895. The event was staged as a tribute to local businessmen and individuals who had contributed toward the purchase of new uniforms.

As the drills became more perfect and the fame of the organization spread beyond the environs of the Grand Traverse Region, the Hannah Rifles were invited to journey to Manistee and take part in a Fourth of July celebration. A record of that day states that the Hannah Rifles were marched with Company B, Fifth regiment, Manistee, and "made as good an appearance as the Manistee Company and all along the line of march were applauded roundly."

In 1898, on December 10, the Hannah Rifles made their first public contribution to entertainment in the region. Heretofore, they had marched in parades, marched on Memorial Day, and had drawn some attendance during their frequent drill sessions.

The entertainment consisted of a full scale program under the patriotic title of "Poetry of the War."

Col. M. A. Aldrich, author of the presentation, came to Traverse City from Grand Rapids to direct the effort. Again a transcript of what happened best describes the event: "The cream of Traverse City's musical talent came readily to the assistance of the citizen soldiers. . . . This was one of the finest musical events ever seen in this city and the merit of the piece, with the popularity of the Hannah Rifles, brought a crowded house." The theme of the show was songs and music of the Civil War.

But the company was still unable to find a place in the National Guard. The excuse offered by those in office was that there was no vacancy. Interest in the civilian-military group, however, remained high. There were a few who became discouraged and dropped out but the membership remained about sixty men.

In the year 1896 there was considerable inside rivalry among the members of the company. The president of the Hannah Rifles had offered a gold medal to the best drilled member of the group and a public parade was held on July 3, 1896. There is no record of which man received the medal but there was a faraway echo of the event.

As a direct result of the excellence of the unit, an inspector, General Case, of the National Guard, and Captain Gardner of the United States Army arrived to inspect the troops. Their report was so excellent that the Hannah Rifles were placed on the list to fill any vacancy which might develop.

But war clouds over Cuba were destined to prevent the entry of the unit into the National Guard. A call for volunteers was issued and the Hannah Rifles responded. There was little difficulty in securing sufficient men to bring the ranks to a complement of eighty-three men by the time they were ready to entrain for Camp Eaton, Island Lake.

That is the story of the growth and development of the Hannah Rifles. How they accounted for themselves in the thick of the Spanish-American War is a repetition of the conduct for which they were so well known at home. They were dependable, capable, and fearless.

It was on February 15, 1898 that the battleship *Maine* was blown up in the harbor at Havana. Then, during the first week in May, 1898, Admiral Dewey destroyed the command of Montejo. This brought war fever and patriotism to a high pitch.

A call for volunteers was received locally (Traverse City) on May 9, 1898. There was no time lost on the part of the members of the Hannah Rifles and the citizenry. A rousing mass meeting was held at the City Opera House and the building was jammed.

The Hannah Rifles sat in a place of honor during the meeting and "listened to words of encouragement and advice from citizens." Perry Hannah was the central figure and delivered a stirring oration.

Again it was Hannah who added spirit to the already fired-

71

up members of the company. He stated that he would pay every member of the company the sum of seven dollars per month for six months in addition to their regular army pay. There wasn't a person in the City Opera House who dreamed that the war could possibly last so long.

The Hannah Rifles left Traverse City on the morning of May 16. The morning dawned with blasting whistles from the "Big Mill," owned by Hannah, Lay and Company, and was joined by every mill and factory in town.

The shrill notes of the fife, and the war-like roll of drums echoed as the entire membership of McPherson Post, G.A.R., marched with the young men to the depot. There was a final roar of gunfire in salute as the train left the station for Camp Eaton. In all, eighty-three members of the company entrained. Mertus Wright, late for the send-off, joined the company at camp, bringing the total to eighty-four men.

At Camp Eaton the unit was joined with additional recruits, bringing the number to 110 and it was this unit, Company M, 34th Michigan Volunteers, which entrained from that place.

The local men in Company M were:

Officers

Captain Joseph V. McIntosh   Second Lieutenant
First Lieutenant Joseph Klassen   Hiram T. Knapp

Sergeants

George Tarbuck   Oscar Thomas
Otto J. Kyselka   Herbert D. Gage
Ruben H. Osborn

Corporals

George Thirlby   Julius C. Johnson
George F. Dago   Quartermaster George B. Doyle
Ralph S. Hastings   Musician Edgar A. Newton
James R. Stables   Wagoner Charles L. Slade
Martin Winnie   Artificer William Bateson

Privates

Cloyd Dalzell
LeRoy Davidson
Alfred Day
Harvey Decker
Hiram A. Dickinson
Wyatt A. Dewitt
Bert Dunham
Frank M. Fuller
Edward E. Garnett
Charles R. Gunton
Ellsworth Hale
Eugene Hargraves
Robt. F. Herkner
Elwyn Hill
Wm. J. Hilliker
Dick H. Hunter
Roland Boughton
Clair Buckner
Wm. E. Clune
C. O. Corbett
Geo. H. Culman
C. C. Vandervorn
Robert E. Walter
Nelson J. Wyckoff
Frank Riley
Wm. R. Roberts
Arthur D. Scott
R. J. Selkirk
J. B. Smedley
Wm. H. Smith
John O. Tatman
Walter T. Thirlby
Grenville Alexander

Ernest C. Irish
Chas. E. Kiplinger
Wm. A. Lafayete
George R. Mather
David J. McMeekin
Carl V. Moody
Don S. Morgan
Wm. H. Nash
Arthur Needham
Amil F. Nerlinger
Geo. R. Newberry
Ernest J. Nichols
Norman O. Palmer
Frank H. Parks
Walter C. Perry
Coliese J. Rasignal
Charles Bootman
Wm. J. Breithaupt
Ernest Cooper
Fred G. Covey
Fred M. Reed
John A. Wood
Jas. C. Woodworth
Mertus E. Wright
John Riley
Ernest Salensky
John W. Scott
Andrew Sleder
Chas. F. Smith
Frank R. Speaman
C. B. Thacker
Verlin C. Thomas

One name which stood out in the ranks of Michigan men involved in the Spanish-American War was Dr. Julius M. Wilhelm, Traverse City. He had enlisted as a private and was promoted to the post of assistant surgeon of the 34th Regiment with the rank of Captain.

When the contingent left training camp, headed for Newport News and Cuba, Lieutenant Knapp was detained to train

73

recruits called to bring the company to full number. Corporals Stables and Dago and Private John Wood also remained at Camp Alger, where the Hannah Rifles were quartered prior to assignment to active duty.

Traverse City recruits, twenty-five of them, who joined Lt. Knapp were:

Daniel B. Huff	Lafayette W. Case
E. J. Henricson	Herbert G. Dean
Ultic J. Lahym	Lee Wrightman
Dominic Chase	Frank D. Nay
Orrin D. Morse	Robert F. Brown
Benj. F. Carlisle	Charles Carpenter
J. Edward Rose	William G. Henry
Peter Johnson	L. E. Henderson
Chas. B. Scofield	Lewis M. Thornson
Jay B. Frazee	Frank Reit
Hans P. Espenson	Allen C. Spafford
Wm. Willard	Irving Cook
John Jessup	

Four members of the Hannah Rifles never returned from Cuba. Under the broiling tropical sun, harried by uncontrollable pests, and living under adverse conditions proved too much for four members of the unit.

Three members of the Hannah Rifles died in July, 1898. They were Frank Fuller, Fred G. Covey, and Grenville Alexander.

George H. Culman, a native of Traverse City, died of disease at Siboney, Cuba on August 9, 1898.

While the Hannah Rifles were in the combat area for considerable time, not one died of gunfire or was even wounded.

There were tales of close escapes, of hazardous duty, ambushed patrols, and other dangers connected with the campaign but not one of the men fell victim to the erratic gunfire of the enemy.

The Hannah Rifles closed their combat career on September 4, 1898. The entire contingent did not return at the same time. They arrived, a few at a time, because illness had hospitalized a number of them and they were detained for treatment. Eventually the entire unit, with the exception of the four who died in Cuba, returned to their homes.

While the Hannah Rifles marched away to whip the Spanish Army, all was not peace and pleasantness at home. There were several outcroppings of strife and political bickering.

One of the most talked-about-for-weeks instances was a scrap which developed between the owners of the Holley and Connable Book Store on East Front Street on one hand, and the city council on the other.

M. B. Holley, one of the partners in the firm, had erected a large bulletin board at the outer edge of the sidewalk and maintained a running account of the war and the welfare of the members of the Hannah Rifles. This was very wrong, according to city code.

Ordered to remove the bulletin board, Holley, a diminutive, well-liked person, sought permission from the council to maintain it temporarily. He was turned down.

On August 18, 1898, Holley attended the regular meeting of the city council, trailing yards of petition bearing the names of nearly a thousand local people. The august body of aldermen meditated thoroughly but briefly and voted a firm "nay." The sign board came down.

Although members of Hannah Rifles were fortunate that no member of their company was injured by enemy fire, many of them fell victim to disease and were returned home, two of them to die shortly thereafter.

". . . Ernest Salensky is very ill at his home five miles from the city. He has a serious case of malaria but it is not necessarily dangerous."

". . . Ralph Hastings is very ill and does not improve perceptibly, although he is receiving the best professional treatment and care."

". . . Robert Herkner is very ill and does not improve rapidly."

75

". . . George Dago is quite sick and unable to leave his residence."

". . . Ed Garnett is quite sick at the home of his brother on Washington street."

". . . Dr. Wilhelm was able to drive out yesterday for the first time since his return from Montauk Point."

". . . Frank Parks and C. O. Corbett are improving very fast."

". . . Julius Johnson was on the street yesterday looking very thin but getting along well."

". . . Ellsworth Hale is improving slowly but surely."

". . . George Tarbuck was somewhat better yesterday."

". . . Walter Thirlby is slowly improving."

Thus it can be seen that the battle was not fought entirely on the soil of Cuba. Within a few days of the return of the Hannah Rifles to Traverse City, two of the members, Cloyd Dalzell and Hiram Dickenson, died and were given military burial at Oakwood Cemetery. As many of the members of the company as could walk marched in solemn parade.

Don Morgan, who was a member of Company M, was a prolific and interesting correspondent. His impressions, dated July 7, 1898, while stationed three miles from Santiago, follow:

"The 34th Michigan Volunteers landed from the *Harvard* about two o'clock Friday, July 1, in a small mining town 15 miles from Santiago. We pitched our tents just outside of the town and soon we ate our first meal upon Cuban soil. The Cuban soldiers and women gathered around, bringing cocoanuts and other Cuban fruits which they exchanged for hardtack or any clothing which we were willing to part with.

"After dinner our ammunition was issued, fifty rounds to each man, and then we had a short time to explore the town, which is much the same as the mining towns in the mountains of Virginia. This part of the island is very mountainous and the rocks are of a peculiar formation, being very porous, and they appear to have been at one time in a molten state. The beach is a shelf of rock running back from the ocean about 500 feet to the mountains. Following along this beach is a narrow gauge railroad which runs to the mines near the city. This road is now being operated by our army.

"As soon as the Massachusetts regiment had landed, we received orders to be ready to march at a moment's notice; and at nine o'clock we commenced our fifteen mile march to Santiago. We reached the headquarters of the 1st Division Army Corps soon after daylight and from there we could plainly hear the noise of the battle which was then taking place on San Juan Hill. After an hour's rest and breakfast at headquarters we resumed our march to the firing line, which we reached about noon. We were quartered upon the side of the hill where the day before one of the most famous charges in history had been made, and we were held as a reserve force, but we were not needed. The firing from the rifle pits continued until dark and then all was quiet until about mid-night, when the Spanish made a desperate attempt to re-capture the hill. They were driven back with heavy loss before they reached our pits.

"At ten o'clock A.M., July 3rd a truce was declared which still continues.

"We celebrated the glorious Fourth by digging trenches in the side of a hill for company quarters, also by a six-mile march to headquarters to recover our blankets and tents which were left there as we came through.

"The general health of the company is excellent, with the exception of Sergeant Tarbuck and Privates McMeekin and Sleder, who are suffering from poison similar to the ivy in Michigan.

"No mail has been received since we left Camp Alger, and we are eagerly looking for news from home.   D. S. Morgan"

Ellsworth Hale, member of the Hannah Rifles, compiled one of the best records. His letters were informative and interesting.

The following letter to his sister was dated at Santiago, Cuba, July 30, 1898:

"My Dear Sister — Yours was the first letter I received on the island and was very welcome. It came on July 11th, three days before the surrender. We were posted on the extreme left supporting the artillery and had a very easy time the last engagement. I happened to be in a very ticklish place in a ravine on guard with two other fellows. We lay flat on the ground with a good fat palm between us and the city for the firing that day was very heavy and bullets were singing all the time.

"We had a very pleasant trip across the water but when we landed, our fun ended. From four o'clock the morning of the first until noon of the next day we were on the march, or move, rather. We marched from nine o'clock that night until 5:30 the next morning when we began to hear the firing and to shake, too, I can assure you. We were under fire by ten o'clock and have been at the front during the rest of it, though it was mostly truce and exchanging terms.

"The scenes I saw during those three or four days, the dead, mangled, and wounded were quite sufficient to give me enough war. In fact, there were hundreds of our own men and Spaniards, too, who fell on the 1st, who laid in the sun and rain until the 5th. I was on a burying detail then and helped to bury three men, two of them 'Rough Riders.' The Spaniards were fairly piled up in their entrenchments and dirt was thrown in on them. But the awful things one sees among the dead and wounded in battle were nothing to those among the starving Cubans. It simply is indescribable. Old men, women, and children by the hundreds were driven from the town of El Caney actually starving. You do not know what that means, I am sure, and neither do I, but we thought we were pretty hungry when we had to live on hard bread and pork several days.

"Now, of course, things are changing but some of the natives drop along the road every day from privation. Our rations are improving now and they give us fresh beef once a day, and all we need to make a home meal is soft bread and butter (which would be soft). We get coffee, mostly green, sugar, potatoes and onions, rice and beans and all the hardtack and pork

78

we can eat. Rice tastes best to me and I'm a past master at cooking it.

"The Spaniards used smokeless powder and it was next to impossible to find them. Maybe it didn't look nice to see our guns, the good old honest kind, crack out and then see a hole put through their blockhouses and watch the Spaniards run out to the tune of a dozen of our Gatlings on the line.

"The Spanish prisoners are all camped out of town and can go in and out as they please. It's mostly in, for the Cubans in the country round are loaded for them. The Spaniards are invariably small, swarthy men, who are too polite for anything. I have traded for lots of things, among them a fine machette, dagger, and a fine silk handkerchief which will be yours provided I do not lose it.

"On the Fourth when you heard the report that I was dead, I wasn't but was engaged most of the forenoon in inserting a large and much needed patch in a hole made by cactus, and in the afternoon by holding it very close to the ground while I thought of home.

"Be sure to write the folks that I'm well and strong. That's straight, too.

Ellsworth Hale"

That, briefly, is the story of the Spanish-American War as it affected the Grand Traverse Region and the story of the flawless record of the Hannah Rifles. Whether digging trenches under a scorching tropical sun or braving enemy fire, the members of the unit carried out their tasks with gallantry and loyalty. They grumbled, found fault with the hardtack and fat pork which they were issued as rations, criticized their officers, and through it all behaved as typical American soldiers and heroes.

Chapter V

MEDICAL ADVICE OF A CENTURY AGO

These choice home remedies are not published with any idea that the head of the household or the warder of the medicine chest will resort to them in case of illness.

Many of them are "Cures" advocated by Dr. T. C. Ware, botanic physician and licentiate of the New Jersey medical staff, published in 1839 as *Wesley's Family Physician Revised* and *Ware's Medical Adviser*.

If you, or a member of your family, are ill, consult your physician; but if you wish to become familiar with some of the medications used a century or more ago, be my guest. Some of the 'Yarbs,' however, are a bit difficult to get at the corner apothecary.

"For An Ague

"Go into a cold bath just before the cold fit.

"Nothing tends more to prolong an ague than indulging a lazy indolent disposition. Between the fits, therefore, the patient ought to take as much exercise as he can bear and to use a light diet. For common drink port wine and water are the most proper.

"One means of curing it is to boil yarrow in new milk 'till it is tender enough to spread a plaster. An hour before the cold fit apply this to the wrists and let it remain 'till the hot fit is over. If another fit comes, use a fresh plaster.

"Another: Pour boiling water on a large spoonful of powdered camomile flowers. When cool, drink it.

"It is proper to take a gentle vomit, and sometimes a purge, before the use of either of the above medicines. If a vomit is taken two hours before the fit is expected, it generally prevents that fit and sometimes cures an ague, especially in children. It is also proper to repeat the medicine (whatever it be), about a week after, in order to prevent a relapse. Do not take any purge after. The daily use of the flesh brush and frequent cold bathing are of great use to prevent relapses.

"Children have been cured by wearing a waistcoat in which bark was quilted."

"St. Anthony's Fire

"St. Anthony's Fire is a fever attended with a red painful swelling, full of pimples which afterwards turn into small blisters on the face or some other part of the body. The sooner the eruption is, the less the danger. Let your diet be only water gruel or barley broth, with roasted apples.

"Take a glass of warm tar-water, in bed, every hour washing the part with the same.

"Tar-water is made thus: Put a gallon of cold water to a quart of Norway tar. Stir them together with a flat stick for five or six minutes. After it has stood covered for three days, pour off the water clear, bottle and cork it.

"Or, take a decoction of elder leaves as a sweat applying to the part a cloth dipped in lime water mixed with a little camphorated spirit of wine.

"Lime water is made thus: Infuse a pound of good quick lime in six quarts of spring water for 24 hours. Decant and keep it for use. Every family should keep this article.

"If the pulse be low and the spirits sunk, nourishing broths and a little negus may be given to advantage. Dressing the inflamation with greasy ointments, salves, etc., is very improper."

"Apoplexy

"To prevent: Use the apoplexy bath, and drink only water.

"In the fit put a handful of salt into a pint of cold water, and if possible, pour it down the throat of the patient. He will quickly come to himself. So will one who seems dead by a fall. But send for a good physician immediately.

"If the fit be soon after a meal, vomit and sweat. A mustard plaster on the neck, with low diet, has often prevented a relapse.

"There is a wide difference between the sanguineous and serious apoplexy. The latter is often followed by a palsy. The former is distinguished by the countenance appearing florid, the face swelled or puffed up, and the blood vessels, especially about the neck and temples, are turgid. The pulse beats strong. The eyes are prominent and fixed; the breathing is difficult and performed with a snorting. This invades more suddenly than the serious apoplexy. Bathe the feet in warm water and pour cold water on the head. The garters should be tied very tight to lessen the motion of the blood from the lower extremities.

"When the patient is so far recovered as to be able to swallow, let him take a cloyster thrown up with plenty of fresh butter, a large spoonful of common salt in it, and pepper.

"In serious apoplexy, the pulse is not so strong; there is great difficulty of breathing. Here bleeding is not necessary but a vomit may be given, and afterwards a purge, as before, and a mustard plaster applied to the back of the neck.

"This apoplexy is generally preceded by an unusual heaviness, giddiness, and drowsiness."

"The Asthma

"Take a pint of cold water every morning, washing the head therein immediately after and using the cold bath once a fortnight.

"Or cut an ounce of stick liquorice into slices. Steep this in a quart of water, four and twenty hours, and use it when you are worse than usual as common drink.

"Or half a pint of tar-water twice a day.

"Or live a fortnight on boiled carrots only. It seldom fails.

"Or take from ten to twenty drops of elixir of vitriol in a glass of water three or four times a day.

"Elixir of vitriol is made thus: Drop gradually four ounces of strong oil of vitriol into a pint of spirits of wine or brandy. Let it stand three days and add to it ginger sliced, half an ounce, and Jamaica pepper, whole, one ounce. In three days more it is fit for use.

"Or into a quart of boiling water put a teaspoonful of balsamic ether. Receive the steam into the lungs through a fumigator twice a day."

"A Dry or Convulsive Asthma

"Juice of radishes relieves much. So does a cup of strong coffee, or garlic, either raw, preserved, or in syrup.

"Drink a pint of new milk morning and evening. This has cured an inveterate asthma.

"Or beat fine saffron small and take eight or ten grains every night.

"Take from three to five grains of ipecacuanha every week. Do this, if need be, for a month or six weeks. Five grains usually vomit. In a violent fit, take fifteen grains.

"In an asthma the best drink is apple water. That is, boiling water poured on sliced apples.

"The food should be light and easy of digestion. Ripe fruits baked, boiled, or roasted, are very proper. Strong liquors of all kinds, especially beer or ale, are hurtful. If any supper is taken, it should be very light."

"To Cure Baldness

"Rub the part morning and evening with onions 'till it is red, and rub it afterwards with honey. Or, wash it with a decoction of box wood."

"Bleeding at the Nose

"To cure it: Apply to the neck, behind and on each side, a cloth dipped in cold water.

"Put the legs and arms in cold water.

"Wash the temples, nose, and neck with vinegar.

"Snuff up vinegar and water.

"Foment the legs and arms with it.

"Steep a linen rag in sharp vinegar, burn it, and blow it up the nose with a quill.

"Apply tents made of soft lint dipped in cold water, strongly impregnated with a solution of alum and introduced within the nostrils.

"Dissolve an ounce of alum powdered in a pint of vinegar; apply a cloth dipped in this to the temples, steeping the feet in cold water.

"In a violent case, go into a pond or river."

"Bleeding of A Wound

"Make two or three tight ligatures towards the lower part of each joint. Slacken them gradually.

"Or apply tops of nettles bruised.

"Or strew on it the ashes of a linen rag dipped in sharp vinegar and burnt.

"Or take ripe puff-balls, break them warily, and save the powder. Strew this on the wound and bind it on. This will stop the bleeding of an amputated limb."

"Blisters

"On the feet, occasioned by walking, are cured by drawing a needleful of worsted through them. Clip it off at both ends and leave it 'till the skin peels off."

"Biles

"Apply a little Venice turpentine.

"Or an equal quantity of soap and brown sugar, well mixed.

"Or a plaster of honey and wheat flour.

"Or a little saffron in a white bread poultice.

"It is proper to purge also."

"A Bruise

"Immediately apply molasses spread on brown paper. Or apply a plaster of chopped parsley mixed with butter."

"A Deep Burn or Scald

"Apply inner rind of elder well mixed with fresh butter. When this is bound on with a rag, plunge the part into cold water. This will suspend the pain 'till the medicine heals.

"Or mix lime water and sweet oil to the thickness of cream. Apply it with a feather several times a day. This is a most effectual application."

"Chin-Cough, or Whooping-Cough

"Rub the feet thoroughly with hog's lard, before the fire, on going to bed, and keep the child warm therein.

"Or rub the back, at lying down, with old rum. It seldom fails.

"Or give a spoonful of juice of penny-royal mixed with brown sugar candy twice a day

"Or half a pint of milk, warm from the cow, with the quantity of a nutmeg or conserve of roses dissolved in it every morning.

"In desperate cases, change of air will have a good effect."

"Cholera Morbus, i.e. Flux and Vomiting of Bile

"Boil a chicken an hour in two gallons of water and drink of this 'till the vomiting ceases.

"Or decoction of rice, or barley, or toasted oatenbread.

"If the pain is very severe, steep the belly with flannels dipped in spirits and water.

"The third day after the cure, take ten or fifteen grains of rhubarb."

"Chopt Hands, (To Prevent)

"Wash them with soft soap mixed with red sand. Or wash them in sugar and water."

"The Cholic, (In The Fit)

"Drink of camomile tea.

"Or take from thirty to forty grains of yellow peel of oranges, dried and powdered in a glass of water.

"Or take from five to six drops of oil of aniseed on a lump of sugar.

"Or apply outwardly a bag of hot oats.

"Or steep the legs in hot water a quarter of an hour.

"Or take as much Daffy's elixir as will presently purge. This relieves the most violent cholic in an hour or two."

"Cholic in Children

"Give a scruple of powdered aniseed in their meat.

"Or small doses of magnesia.

"Or a drachm of anisated tincture of rhubarb every three hours 'till it operates."

"A Nervous Cholic

"Use the cold bath daily for three or four weeks.

"In the fit, drink fresh melted butter and then vomit with warm water.

"To prevent or cure. Breakfast daily on fat broth, and use oil of sweet almonds frequently

"Smelters of metals, plummers, etc. may be in a good measure preserved from the poisonous fumes that surround them by breathing through cloth or flannel mufflers two or three fold, dipped in a solution of sea-salt, or salt of tartar, and then dried. These mufflers might also be of great use in many similar cases."

"Windy Cholic

"Parched peas, eaten freely, have had the most happy effects when all other means had failed."

"To Prevent the Ill-Effects of Cold

"The moment a person gets into the house with his hands and feet quite chilled, let him put them into a vessel of water as cold as can be got and hold them there 'till they begin to glow. This they will do in a minute or two. This method likewise effectually prevents chilblains."

"A Consumption

"One in a deep consumption was advised to drink nothing but water, and eat nothing but water-gruel without salt or sugar. In three months time he was perfectly well.

"Take no food but new butter-milk, churned in a bottle, and white bread

"Or use as common drink, spring water and new milk, each a quart, and sugar candy two ounces.

"Or boil two handfuls of sorrel in a pint of whey. Strain it and drink a glass twice a day

"Or turn a pint of skimmed milk with half a pint of small beer. Boil in this whey about twenty ivy-leaves and two or three sprigs of hyssop. Drink half over night, the rest in the morning. Do this, if needful, for two months daily. This has cured in a desperate case.

"Or breathe the pure morning dew.

"Or throw frankincense in burning coals, and receive the smoke daily through a proper tube into the lungs.

"Or take in, for a quarter of an hour, morning and evening, the steam of white rosin and beeswax boiling on a hot fire-shovel. This has cured one who was in the third stage of a consumption.

"Or the steam of sweet spirit of vitriol dropped into warm water.

"Or drink thrice a day two spoonfuls of juice of water-cresses. This has cured a deep consumption."

"Convulsions

"Use the cold bath.

"Or take a teaspoonful of valerian root (nerve powder) powdered in a cup of water every evening.

88

"Or half a drachm of mistletoe, powdered, every six hours, drinking after it a draught of strong infusion thereof."

"Corns, (To Prevent)

"Frequently wash the feet in cold water."

"Corns, (To Cure)

"Apply fresh every morning the yeast of small beer spread on a rag.

"Or after paring them close, apply bruised ivy-leaves daily, and in fifteen days they will drop out.

"Some corns are cured by a pitch plaster."

"The Cramp, (To Prevent)

"Tie your garter smooth and tight under your knee at going to bed.

"Or take half a pint of tar-water morning and evening.

"Or to one ounce and a half of spirits of turpentine, add flour of brimstone and sulphur of each half an ounce. Smell it at night three or four times."

"The Dropsy

"Use the cold bath daily, after purging.

"Or rub the swelled parts with salad-oil by a warm hand at least an hour a day. This has done wonders in some cases.

"Or cover the whole belly with a large new sponge dipped in strong lime-water and then squeezed out. This bound on often cures even without any sensible evacuation of water.

"Or apply green dock-leaves to the joints and soles of the feet, changing them once a day.

"Or eat a crust of bread every morning fasting.

"Tar-water drank twice a day has cured many; so has an infusion of juniper berries roasted and made into a liquor like coffee.

"Or three spoonfuls of the juice of leeks or elderleaves.

"Or of the decoction of the tops of oak boughs. This cured an inveterate dropsy in fifteen days."

"*The Ear-Ache Without Inflamation*

"Rub the ear hard a quarter of an hour.

"Or put in a roasted fig, or onion, as hot as may be.

"Or blow the smoke of tobacco strongly into it.

"But if the ear-ache is caused by an inflamation of the uvula, it is cured in two or three hours by receiving into the mouth the steam of bruised hemp-seed boiled in water."

"*Blood-Shot Eye*

"Apply linen rags dipped in cold water two or three hours.

"Or blow in white sugar candy, finely powdered."

"*Clouds Flying Before the Eye*

"Take a drachm of powdered betony every morning."

"*Dull Sight*

"Drop in two or three drops of juice of rotten apples often."

"*Films*

"Mix juice of ground ivy with a little honey and two or three grains of bay-salt. Drop it in morning and evening."

"*Eyes or Eye-Lids Inflamed*

"Apply as a poultice boiled, roasted, or rotten apples warm.

"Or wormwood tops with the yolk of an egg: This will hardly fail."

"*Weak Eyes*

"Wash the head daily with cold water.

"Or take of white vitroil half a drachm, rose water six ounces to dissolve it, and filter the water to touch the eye often.

The temples and round the eye may be touched with camphorated spirits.

"If the eyes are inflamed, the patient should have mustard plasters behind the ears and on the back of the neck."

"A Fever

"Drink a pint and half of cold water lying down in bed.

"To prevent catching any infectious fever, do not breathe near the face of a sick person, neither swallow your spittle while in the room. Infection seizes the stomach first."

"The Gout in the Foot or Hand

"Apply a raw, lean steak. Change it once in twelve hours until cured.

"Rub the part with warm treacle, and then bind on a flannel smeared therewith. Repeat this, if need be, once in twelve hours.

"Or drink a pint of strong infusion of elder buds, dry or green, morning and evening. This has cured inveterate gouts.

"Or at six in the evening, undress and wrap yourself up in blankets. Then put your legs up to the knees in water as hot as you can bear it. As it cools, let hot water be poured in so as to keep you in a strong sweat 'till ten. Then go into a bed well warmed, and sweat 'till morning."

"The Green Sickness

"Take a cup of decoction of lignum guaiacum, (commonly called lignum vitae) morning and evening. Use the hot bath every night."

"The Head-Ache

"Rub the head for a quarter of an hour.

"Or pour upon the palm of the hand a little brandy and some zest of lemon, and hold it to the forehead.

"Or apply to each temple the thin yellow rind of a lemon, newly pared off.

"Or a little juice of horse radish.

"Take a vomit."

"A Hemicrania

"Use cold bathing.

"Or apply to that part of the head, on the temples, a mustard plaster."

"The Heart-Burning

"Drink a pint of cold water.

"Or drink slowly a decoction of camomile flowers.

"Or a teaspoonful of magnesia.

"Or chew five or six pepper-corns a little, then swallow them.

"Or chew fennel or parsley and swallow your spittle. Sometimes a vomit is needful.

"Or a piece of Spanish liquorice.

"Or a teaspoonful of chalk in water."

"Hiccough, (To Cure)

"Swallow a mouthful of water, stopping the mouth and ears.

"Or take anything that makes you sneeze.

"Or two or three preserved damsons.

"Or three drops of oil of cinnamon on a lump of sugar.

"Or ten drops of chemical oil of amber dropped on sugar and then mixed with a little water."

"Hoarseness

"Rub the soles of the feet before the fire with garlic and lard well beaten together, overnight. The hoarseness will be gone next morning.

"Or swallow slowly the juice of radishes.

"Or half a pint of mustard-whey lying down.

"Or dry nettle roots in an oven, powder them finely, and mix with an equal quantity of treacle. Take a spoonful of this twice a day."

"The Jaundice

"Take a small pill of Castile soap every morning for eight or ten days."

"The Itch

"Wash the parts affected with strong rum.

"Or anoint them with black soap.

"Or steep a shirt half an hour in a quart of water mixed with half an ounce of powdered brimstone. Dry it slowly, and wear it five or six days. Sometimes it needs repeating."

"Lice, (To Kill)

"Sprinkle Spanish snuff over the head.

"For One Seemingly Killed by Lightning, A Damp, or Suffocated

"Plunge him immediately into cold water.

"Or blow strongly with bellows down his throat. This may recover a person seemingly drowned. It is still better if a strong man blows into his mouth."

"Lunacy

"Rub the head several times a day with vinegar in which ground ivy-leaves have been infused.

"Or take daily an ounce of distilled vinegar.

"Or boil juice of ground ivy with sweet oil and white wine into an ointment. Shave the head, anoint it therewith, and chafe it in warm water every other day for three weeks. Bruise also the leaves and bind them on the head and give three spoonfuls of the juice, warm, every morning. This generally cures melancholy."

"Raging Madness

"Sit the patient under a great waterfall as long as his strength will bear. Or pour water on his head out of a tea-kettle.

"Let him eat nothing but bread and milk and ripe fruit."

"The Bite of A Mad Dog

"Plunge into cold water daily for twenty days and keep as long under it as possible. This has cured even after the hydrophobia was begun.

"Or mix ashes of trefoil, or oak ashes, with hog's lard and anoint the part as soon as possible; repeat twice or thrice at six hours intervention.

"Or take two or three spoonfuls of the juice of ribwort, morning and evening, as soon as possible after the bite. Repeat this for two or three changes of the moon. It has not been known to fail."

"The Measles

"Immediately consult an honest physician.

"Drink only thin water-gruel or milk and water, the more the better, or toast and water.

"If the cough be very troublesome, take frequently a spoonful of barley water, sweetened with oil of new almonds newly drawn, mixed with syrup.

"After the measles, take three or four purges and for some weeks take care of taking cold, use light diet, and drink barley water instead of malt drink."

"To Make Milk Agree with the Stomach

"If it lie heavy, put a little salt in it. If it curdle, sugar. For bilious persons mix it with water."

"Nettle Rash, or Prickly Heat

"Rub the parts strongly with parsley, or salt and water."

"Beating of the Heart

"Apply outwardly a rag dipped in vinegar.
"Or take a decoction of mother's wort every night."

"The Pleurisy

"Use a decoction of nettles; and apply the boiled herb hot
as a poultice.
"Or a plaster of flour of brimstone and white of an egg."

"The Rheumatism

"To prevent. Wear washed wool under the feet.
"To cure. Live on new milk-whey and white bread for
fourteen days. This has cured in a desperate case.
"Or pound the green stalks of English rhubarb, in May or
June, with an equal quantity of lump sugar. Take the quantity
of a nutmeg of this three or four times a day.
"In a stubborn rheumatism, let your diet be barley gruel
with currants, roasted apples, fresh whey, and light pudding."

"To Restore the Strength After A Rheumatism

"Make a strong broth of cow-heels, and wash the parts with
it, warm, twice a day. It has restored one who was quite a cripple,
having no strength left either in his thigh, leg, or loins."

"Ring Worms

"Apply rotten apples or pounded garlic.
"Or rub them with the juice of house leek.
"Or twice a day with oil of sweet almonds and oil of tartar
mixed."

"A Broken Shin

"Bind a dry oak leaf upon it.
"Or put on a bit of white paper moistened with spittle. It
will stay on 'till the place is well.
"This cures a cut also."

"Shingles

"Drink sea water or salt water every morning for a week. Toward the close, bathe.

"Or apply pounded garlic."

"Small Pox

"Drink largely of toast and water.

"Or let your whole food be milk and water mixed with a little white bread.

"Or milk and apples."

"A Venomous Sting

"Apply the juice of honey-suckle leaves.

"Or a poultice of bruised plantain and honey.

"Or take inwardly one drachm of black currant leaves powdered. It is an excellent counter-poison."

"The Sting Of A Bee

"Apply honey."

"The Sting Of A Nettle

"Rub the part with juice of nettles."

"The Sting Of A Wasp

"Rub the part with the bruised leaves of the house leek, water cresses, or rue.

"Or apply molasses or sweet oil.

"Or, bruised onions or garlic."

"Sting in the Gullet

"Beat well together with a spoon some honey and sweet oil with a little vinegar; swallow a spoonful every minute 'till ease is obtained."

"A Stitch in the Side

"Apply molasses spread on hot toast."

"Accidental Sickness or Pain in the Stomach
"Vomit with a quart of warm water."

"Twisting of the Bowels
"Use injection of tobacco smoke."

"Tympany, or Windy Dropsy
"Use the cold bath with purges intermixed.
"Or mix the juice of leeks and of elder. Take two or three spoonfuls of this morning and evening.
"Or eat a few parched peas every hour."

"Bite of a Viper or Rattlesnake
"Apply bruised garlic.
"Or rub the place immediately with common oil.
"Or apply the liver and guts of the serpent to the wound. Good in the bite of any serpent."

Chapter VI

PROEM

History records that Washington was the first president of these United States and legend has it that he couldn't tell a lie if there was a possibility he would get caught at it.

The story of Nero and his violin and the yarn about Robert the Bruce and his fortune-telling spider are well known to most youngsters and grown-ups. The recorded history of the Civil War, of World War II, and of the sinking of the *Maine* are a part of modern text books.

How many teenagers, betweenagers, and adults today can remember the run-of-the-mill news stories which were the fare of the folks of a half century or a century ago?

Who can discuss the western migration of the hardy people of three quarters of a century ago? Who can tell about Carrie Nation and her nasty little hatchet?

Not many of we moderns can recall any of the "little things" which were so vital to the work-a-day world of yesterday.

Here are some of the stories from newspapers of the past; stories which were deemed worthy of comment. It will be noted that, in many instances, editorial opinion was incorporated into the stories. This is in direct contrast to the modern journalistic approach, wherein news stories are kept as unbiased and free from opinion as possible. Today the use of the word "Democrat" without using the word "Republican" in the same story is to court a demand for "equal time."

"*A Word To Emigrants*

"Traverse City, Michigan, November 26, 1858.

"To the thousands of hardy and enterprising men who will be seeking new homes in the great west next spring, we can confidently say that the northern Michigan country offers stronger and better inducements than either Illinois, Wisconsin, Iowa, or Minnesota.

"To the farmer, especially, we say, come and see. There is no more healthy country on the habitable globe. The climate is as fine and salubrious as can be found in the same parallel of latitude in North America. The soil is as rich and productive as that of any timbered country we ever saw. It is well watered, abounding in beautiful lakes, rivers, and brooklets filled with trout, pickerel, and bass; and the timber (chiefly hard maple, beech, white oak, ash, basswood, and elm) is large and thrifty.

"We have no early frosts to injure crops; and the lowest range of the thermometer this fall, up to the 25th of November, has been 28 degrees above zero. We have a bay 40 miles long by 10 broad, with a dozen or more safe and commodious natural harbors.

"Immense tracts of the very best farming lands are still owned by the government and can be bought for $1.25 per acre. The land office is located at Traverse City, the county seat of Grand Traverse county, and every facility is afforded to those desirous of making locations.

"A heavy lumbering business now is, and for many years to come, will be transacted on the bay. Though there is very little pine in the immediate vicinity, yet some thirty or forty miles in the interior there are vast forests of pine timber, which is cut in winter and floated down the various tributaries of the bay in the spring. Here it is sawed into lumber during the summer and shipped to Chicago.

"There is a good home market at fair prices for all the surplus produce which will be raised for the next ten years; and when the supply shall become greater than the home demand, the farmer can have his choice of markets abroad without being subject to the expense of land transportation for one, two, three, and four hundred miles before he can ship it to tidewater, as is the case in Iowa and Minnesota and in some parts of Illinois and Wisconsin.

100

"Twenty thousand farmers may settle in the counties bordering Grand Traverse bay, and not one of them have to carry his produce over ten miles to ship it to Buffalo or Chicago.

"Can any western state or territory offer more favorable inducements to the emigrant farmer?"

"Attempt To Commit Murder

"Traverse City, Michigan, July 11, 1862.

"An attempt was made to murder James K. Gunton, proprietor of the Gunton House in Traverse City, on the night of the fourth by E. F. French, who came to this place about a month ago from Greenville in Montcalm county, with the avowed object of establishing a land agency here, a business in which he had been engaged for some years at Greenville and where, if his statements are to be relied upon, he established a wide and enviable reputation as a prompt and energetic man. His career here was more brief than brilliant.

"The circumstances connected with his attempt to murder Mr. Gunton are these: He had been indulging freely in ale during the afternoon and evening and finally became noisy and quarrelsome. His wife called at the house and tried to persuade him to go home. He refused to accompany her and applied to her abusive and indecorous epithets, which induced Mr. Gunton to request him to leave his house.

"Sharp words followed, when Mr. French left, threatening soon to return and 'attend to Mr. Gunton's case.' He repaired immediately to his own house, (a short distance from the Gunton House) took down a double-barreled rifle, and told his wife that he was going to shoot Gunton.

"The screams of the wife were heard at the Gunton house, and three or four men repaired immediately to French's house. They found him armed with the rifle and threatening loudly to kill Gunton before morning. After talking with him for some time, he promised them that he would postpone the execution of his threat until morning, and they left him.

101

"As soon as they were gone, he told his wife that he should put his threat into immediate execution. He requested her to sell her furniture, disinter the body of her child which had died about three weeks before, take it back to Greenville, and return herself to her parents at Grand Haven, threatening at the same time to shoot her on the spot if she made any further resistance to his carrying out his plan to murder Gunton.

"He proceeded immediately towards the Gunton House, took deliberate aim at Gunton through a window, and fired. The gun was discharged with slugs. A glass sugar dish and a water pitcher were standing on the counter over which Gunton was leaning, and between him and the window. They received the contents of the gun and were shattered in a thousand pieces, only one of the slugs striking Mr. Gunton on the arm and inflicting a slight wound.

"But for these intervening objects, Mr. Gunton would have been shot directly through the body and instantly killed. French then took to the woods, armed with a rifle, revolver, and Bowie knife. He was seen the next morning at 4:00 o'clock, seven miles from town, and has doubtless taken the old Indian trail to Saginaw. The sheriff and Mr. Gunton have gone in pursuit of him. [Author's note: They never caught up with French.]"

"Woman Shipped In A Box

"Ryegate, Vermont, January 6, 1865.

"A live woman is on her way from Ryegate, Vermont, to San Francisco in a closed pine box, about the size of a coffin. She has a nervous affection of the brain and this mode of transportation was resorted to, to protect her from the noise incident to the journey. The box has a small aperture to admit air, contains a bed, and is muffled. On stopping for the night, she exchanges her coffin for a bed.

"Prolific

"Chicago, Illinois, January 6, 1865.

"We met a widow woman yesterday, only twenty-one years old, and yet the mother of eleven children. She was a refugee from Tennessee and married when she was but fifteen years old, and in nine months thereafter was the mother of three live, healthy children.

"In the next twelve months, she gave birth to twin girls; then, inside the next twelve months, she was the mother of triplets again, two boys and girl. After a pause of eighteen months, she presented her husband with another round of triplets, two girls and a boy, and she arrived in our city with the entire lot.

"Her husband lost his life at the Battle of Stone River and she, with her interesting and bright-eyed, merry little group, were left to find their way, upon the charity of other people, to her friends in the middle portion of Illinois where she expected to be placed beyond all such humiliating necessities.

"Her short life has been eventful as well as prolific of events. She looks remarkably young and active and if there is no preventing providence, we will go security on her some day, securing the town in which she located from all draft for the army."

"Row in a Detroit Church

"Detroit, Michigan, February 16, 1866.

"On Monday night, January 26th, a disgraceful riot occurred in a church in this city. It appears that there is a school in the church which is attended by the children of the congregation.

"The pastor of the church has a scapegrace son attending the school. A short time since this boy was detected in writing anonymous letters of a disgraceful character to several of the girls who attended the school. The teacher became very much incensed at this conduct of the boy and administered a severe castigation to him.

103

"This whipping was the cause of all the trouble and so much enraged the minister that he is said to have sworn a big oath against the teacher and straightway ousted him from his position.

"This caused the members of the congregation to assemble in full strength, 150 in number, resolved on defending and sustaining the teacher, and equally firm in their determination to kick the reverend out of the church.

"The matter was discussed, at first calmly, but soon passion predominated and things began to look squally.

"About 9:00 o'clock the meeting could not be controlled, and it was found impossible to restore order. An attempt was made to offer violence to the person of the pastor and the excitement was intense.

"The outraged females were the most violent in their rage and it is reported that several of them drew long, gleaming butcherknives, which they had brought there for the purpose, and brandishing them threateningly over their heads declared their intention to execute summary vengeance upon the object of their hatred.

"At this stage of the proceedings the police were sent for and five or six of the guardians of the city's peace arrived while the turmoil and excitement was at its height.

"With drawn clubs the police succeeded in driving back the mob. As they passed the excited crowd, the females were almost wild with rage and uttered fearful maledictions. Some of them attempted to grapple with their pastor, and a large number spat towards and upon him as he passed.

"Under the protection of the police he was finally taken to his residence and the congregation dispersed in knots."

"Lost and Found

"Jackson, Michigan, October 26, 1866.

"Thirty years ago, when Jackson was a little hamlet of two or three hundred persons, a young woman might have been seen one sultry day in August, accompanied by a little boy five years old, wending her way towards a grove in the neighboring town of Blackman for the purpose of engaging in the then common pastime of picking berries.

"The young woman, after toiling away for awhile, became annoyed with the ceaseless importunities of the child and sent him home. She thought nothing more of the matter until, upon her return in the evening, she was surprised to find that the boy had not returned.

"In reply to the queries of the anxious parents the girl related the circumstances narrated above, adding that she knew nothing of the whereabouts of the child.

"Day after day passed and still the missing member of that distracted family did not return, nor could any tidings of him be heard by his agonized parents. Finally after every searching party who went out to find the missing one had returned and reported their mission fruitless, and after all hope of ever seeing their darling boy again had vanished from the minds of the afflicted parents, suspicion began to fasten upon the young woman, who was a servant in the family.

"She again asserted her innocence and stated that she knew nothing of the missing boy from the time she had sent him homeward. In spite of her protests, she was arrested for the murder of the boy and put in the rude lock-up which had been erected by the early settlers. Here she was kept for a time until it became apparent that no evidence against her could be obtained, when she was discharged from custody still asserting her innocence to the parents of the child, who longed for some tidings that would dispel the uncertainty which hung over them like a cloud.

"Their hopes were doomed to disappointment, however, as nothing could be heard of the missing one, and he was finally numbered with the dead, the parents giving up all hopes of ever hearing from their lost boy again.

"Years passed and the little hamlet became a flourishing city. The solitude which formerly reigned on the banks of the

Grand river was broken by the mechanic and the artisan, and the air resounded with the busy hum of industry.

"Nearly all the old settlers had passed away and another generation succeeded them. Among the many new comers was a son-in-law of the afflicted family, Mr. J. Z. Ballard, our fellow townsman, who was greatly surprised a few days since to learn that the boy who had long been numbered with the dead had arrived in the southern part of this state and was making inquiries about his family.

"The boy had grown to be a stalwart man of thirty-five. His countenance had become bronzed by continued exposure to the elements and his sinewy frame hardened by repeated adventures in the western wilds.

"He stated that he had but a dim recollection of his former home but vividly remembered the time when two stalwart forms with red visages crossed his path, snatched him up in their arms, and carried him off amidst his piteous cries for his loving mother.

"Since that time he has been constantly with the Indians, joined them in their hunting expeditions, and followed their trail as they journeyed toward the setting sun. He learned to speak the language of the Pottawatomies for that was the name of the tribe with whom the greater part of his life had been spent. In answer to his repeated inquiries his captors told him that they had stolen him from Jackson county and that his name was Willey. The Indians confounded this name with Filly, which is the real name of his father. Mr. Ballard went in quest of the missing one and upon arriving at the place where he had been making inquiries, was told that he had gone away but would return in a few days when he will proceed to the home of his aged parents to make glad the hearts of an afflicted father and mother. Surely, truth is stranger than fiction."

"Narrow Escape

"Taylorsville, Tennessee, November 2, 1866.
"A subscriber living in the neighborhood of Taylorsville

has given us the particulars of an accident which promised to be most unfortunate in its results, but in which the victim was providentially saved.

"It seems that there was a meeting in progress at a church near Taylorsville and the lady in question, together with a male friend, was on her way to attend it.

"The couple were walking leisurely along the road when, to the horror and dismay of the gentleman, the lady, Miss Ellen Sorey, suddenly disappeared in the earth.

"Recovering as quickly as possible from surprise, the gentleman commenced a search for his missing companion and hearing sounds which seemed to come from the bowels of the earth, he soon discovered that she had fallen into a cavern which turned out to be eighty feet deep.

"Assistance was rendered by persons living in the immediate vicinity as quickly as possible by letting bedcords into the hole, and after much labor the lady was hauled up, to the gratification of her friends, very little injured.

"The cavern into which Miss Sorey had fallen is a fearful place, being about three feet in circumference at its mouth and eighty feet deep. Fortunately, she caught on a ledge before reaching the bottom and was therefore saved."

"A Pillar of Fire

"Nashville, Tennessee, August 26, 1869.

"The most curious phenomenon which we have ever heard of occurred out in Chetham county a few days since. The day, it will be remembered, was remarkably hot so that most people in the country had to seek the shade at noon.

"At this hour on the farm of Edward Sharp, five miles from Ashland, a sort of whirlwind came along over the neighboring woods taking up small branches and leaves of trees and burning them in a sort of flaming cylinder that traveled at the rate of about five miles an hour, and developing size as it traveled.

"It passed directly over the spot where a team of horses were feeding and singed their manes and tails up to the roots.

107

It then swept towards the house, taking a stack of hay in its course. It seemed to increase in heat as it went and by the time it reached the house, immediately fired the shingles from end to end of the building. In ten minutes the whole dwelling was wrapped in flames.

"The tall column of traveling caloric then continued its course over a wheat field that had recently been cradled, setting fire to all the shocks that happened to be in its course.

"Passing from the field, its path lay over a stretch of woods which reached the river. The green leaves on the trees were crisped to a cinder for a breadth of twenty yards in a straight line to the Cumberland.

"When the 'pillar of fire' reached the water, it suddenly changed its route down the river raising a column of steam which went up to the clouds for about half a mile, when it finally died out.

"Not less than two hundred people witnessed this strangest of strange phenomenons and all of them tell substantially the same story about it."

"The farmer, Sharp, was left houseless by the devouring elements and his two horses were so affected that no good is expected to be got out of them in the future. Several withered trees in the woods through which it passed were set on fire and continue burning still."

"State Fair at Kalamazoo

"Kalamazoo, Michigan, September 28, 1871.

The State Fair at Kalamazoo was a grand success. In display and attendance it eclipses all former exhibitions. On Thursday the attendance was estimated by good judges to be about 25,000 and the receipts at the gates indicated about this number. The grounds are spacious, and well fitted up, and well provided with buildings and a mile track in very good condition.

"In comparison with the Union Fair held in Traverse City last week, each had points of superiority. In the display of fruit and carriages, the Union Fair was acknowledged to be, by good

108

judges, far ahead of the display at Kalamazoo. Of farm and other machinery, much the larger display was made at the State Fair. The display of stock was about equal if we except the extraordinary display of cattle made at the State Fair, which was very large, and probably as good as was ever seen anywhere.

"Floral Hall, a large building was filled full with rich and beautiful goods, and was ornamented with pictures not entered for exhibition but loaned by the citizens of Kalamazoo for the purpose to a committee of citizens to look after the matter. In the center of the building was a fountain supplied with water from the Holly works."

"Fire in Manistee

"Manistee, Michigan, October 19, 1871.

"Three-fourths of the city of Manistee is in ashes. The wind blew a heavy gale all day yesterday and fire caught in different parts of the city. The fire company worked all day near Glifford and Ruddock's Mill and succeeded in staying the force of the fire there, when the alarm called them to Mr. Canfield's Mill in quite another part of town. The engine gave out about ten o'clock and during the balance of the night was hors de combat.

"The wind blew fearfully and in a short time Canfield's Mill, with all the adjoining buildings and light house, were in flames, the flames licking up in their fearful ravages every vestige of combustible material.

"While the fire was yet burning wildly in that direction, it was discovered that fire had broken out in J. G. Ramsdell's residence, and in less than half an hour the burning sawdust had reached every dwelling on the street as far as the river and all were in flames.

"The loss will be over $2,000,000, a great proportion of which is not insured. There are about 1,200 families homeless and houseless. The churches, school houses, boarding houses, hotels, and every available space is thrown open for the use of the homeless.

"The fire has made a clean sweep from Oak Street to the Little Lake, Cushman, Calkin's and Company's property on the north side is totally destroyed. The bridge, the schooner Seneca Chief, and another schooner are burned. The fire is still raging and if the wind does not go down soon, the rest of the city is in danger of sharing a like fate, and all retreat seems to be cut off as the country is on fire for several miles around.

"Any assistance from neighboring towns will be thankfully received for the people who are, at this season, turned into a burning desolate street. In the hurry, confusion, smoke, and consternation that prevails, we will not attempt further paritculars at present."

"New Capitol Building

"Lansing, Michigan, March 14, 1872.

"Among the important matters likely to claim the attention of the legislature at the session which commenced on the 13th is the law providing for the building of our new state capitol. As the law now stands, the work must necessarily be let in 'piece-meal contracts' as a few thousand or a few hundred thousand dollars are raised from year to year to carry it forward. If built in this way, the new state house will doubtless cost some hundreds of thousands dollars more than if let in a single job.

"The Board of Building Commissioners, it is said, after a careful examination of the whole matter, has come to the conclusion that the piece-meal method will not work and that the entire job should be embraced in a single contract. It is understood that the Board has asked the Governor to bring the subject before the legislature and recommend such a change of the law as is necessary to effect the object sought.

"As a sound, practical, business man, there is no doubt he will do it. It is the only way in which a work of this kind can be properly done and for a fair compensation.

"The building of the capitol will doubtless occupy three or four years. During that period sufficient money can be raised

110

to pay for the work as it progresses. Under our state constitution, bonds cannot be issued. The amount necessary can be raised by the time the building is completed without serious inconvenience.

"It is believed that the Governor will bring this matter before the legislature, that the necessary change in the law will be made clothing the Board of Building Commissioners with all proper authority, and that provision will also be made for raising money to pay for the work as it progresses."

"Insect Plague

"Kansas City, Missouri, June 3, 1875.

"Thousands of people have been reading from day to day the grasshopper reports from Minnesota, Nebraska, Kansas, and Missouri. So destructive were these pests in some of the above named states last year, and so numerous were they represented to be in all of them a few weeks since, that a deep interest in regard to the matter had been awakened all over the land.

"Considerable alarm, for which there seemed to be good reason, was felt throughout all the prairie states of the west. It was even predicted, and feared, that Illinois, and perhaps states even farther east, would not escape their ravages.

"In Missouri the governor appointed Tuesday, June 3, as a day of fasting and prayer, as the danger seemed to be so great that nothing less than Divine Providence could be expected to turn it aside. The feeling generally, however, seemed to be that 'faith without works' would not destroy the pests, and so, throughout the grasshopper regions, the people have been fighting them as if for dear life.

"Millions upon millions of them have been crushed beneath heavy rollers passed over the ground; countless myriads have been burned with grass and straw; and thousands of bushels of them have been driven into ditches and then burned or buried.

"Finally Providence seems to have come to the aid of those who were proving their faith by their works, and a terrible and unexpected slaughter of grasshoppers has occurred.

111

"At the present a parasite, a small red fly, is said to be making havoc with the grasshoppers in Kansas. It appears to have been created especially for this beneficent service. It is the natural enemy of the voracious hopper, and strikes only to kill. It lights upon the grasshopper as he flies and deposits somewhere about his capacious abdomen a single egg. This egg speedily hatches in the form of a small black worm resembling the common grub, which eats its way into the grasshopper's vitals, and then, abandoning the corpse, goes into the ground and reappears after a few days in the shape of a new parasitic fly.

"The number of grasshoppers already 'laid out' by this little instrument of destiny is beyond computation, even in dry measure. In some localities there are regular windrows of the slain, each one with a fatal hole in his bowels and a worm at work on his inner remains. The scientists say that the appearance of this fly closes the career of the present crop of grasshoppers, in which case not Kansas, Nebraska, and Missouri alone, but Iowa, Illinois, Kentucky, Arkansas, and other states still further east and south as well, will have cause to rise and sing for it will mean deliverance from a peril second in awfulness to none other that ever menaced the industry and well being of any people.

"But the 'red fly' does not work alone in the grasshopper killing business. On the 27th of last month, an unusually heavy rain fell over large portions of Missouri, Kansas, and Nebraska, which, while it did some damage, is believed to have been of incalculable benefit in the destruction of grasshoppers.

" 'Untold millions of these insects,' says a report from Kansas City, 'have been destroyed by the flood; they were washed into the gutters and sewers in this city, and the streams in this vicinity have been full of them today.

" 'The Missouri river, opposite the city, has been black with them, and there is hardly any estimating the number that have floated past. The levee has been visited by hundreds of people to view the gratifying sight. There is no question but what the bulk of the insects in this vicinity have been destroyed by the flood, and if it continues through tonight, as there is every prospect, there will be few left to trouble the farmers. In the open fields the ground, in places, is thick with dead hoppers that have been killed by the beating rain. The feeling of dread is rapidly giving way to one of rejoicing, and Governor Hardin will doubtless be called on to issue a proclamation of thanksgiving instead of one of fasting and prayer.'

"Similar reports come from other quarters, and it seems highly probable that the danger of any serious and widespread destruction of crops by grasshoppers is much less than it was ten days ago."

"Daring Robbery

"Traverse City, June 1, 1876.

"Last night some person or persons entered the United States Express Office in this village, opened the safe, and stole therefrom about $2,000 in money. The particulars, as we learn them, are as follows:

"The agent, E. W. Garretson, lives in a large two-story house on Boardman avenue. His sleeping room is on the second floor, one of the windows opening upon a flat roofed piazza. There was a social gathering at the house last evening and in consequence, it was quite late when Mr. Garretson and his wife retired.

"This morning it was found that someone had climbed to the roof of the piazza, removed the wire screen from the window, entered the bedroom, and taken the keys of the safe from the pocket of Mr. Garretson's pants. A burnt scrap of paper that had been used as a light was found on the floor and the pants were lying partly on the roof. At once alarmed, Mr. Garretson hastened to the office and found the front window near the safe open and the safe unlocked, keys still in it, and upon examination discovered that money and money packages to the value of about $2,000 had been taken.

"The safe has no combination lock, and it was therefore an easy matter for any one to open it if he could become possessed of the keys. No clue has been obtained to the burglars."

"Severe Winter

"St. Paul, Minnesota, February 10, 1881.

"The winter is terribly severe in the far northwest, and the greatest suffering and destitution exist. A St. Paul despatch of the 5th thus pictures the fearful condition of the settlers and farmers along the line of the Winona and St. Peter's railroad: 'On Wednesday last, Mr. Burke, the roadmaster, while working with his men near Burke's station, noticed a shanty close by from which no smoke issued. Seeing evidences that the shanty was inhabited, the party visited the place and forced upon the door. Upon a squalid couch on the floor of the wretched hovel lay father, mother, and children, evidently a whole family, frozen to death.

"It is stated that no trains carrying fuel have passed Sleepy Eye Station since December 24th. The country is a broad expanse of prairie, with hardly a stick of timber within miles of the railroad. Settlers have rushed in, taken claims; and, deluded by the mild winters of the past few years, have not made sufficient provision against the severe cold of the past few months.

"They have been obliged to burn furniture, fencing, pieces of boards from their houses, and even the woodwork of their farm machinery. Many of the country roads are utterly impassable and if wood was plenty on the line of the railroad, it could not be got to many of the sufferers. It is feared that many of them will starve or freeze to death before assistance can reach them."

"The Great Storm

"Traverse City, Michigan, March 3, 1881.

"The storm of Sunday night and Monday was probably the worst of its kind ever known here. Rain fell heavily most of the day Saturday and continued up to Sunday afternoon. Snow then began falling, the wind increased to a hurricane, and the night was wild indeed.

"Monday morning the scene was one of grandeur and wild tumult. The wind continued a hard gale from the north, the snow fell rapidly, but no man could tell how rapidly for the air was full of drifting, driving snow flakes and snow drifts. One could see objects but a few feet distant.

"The snow was piled high in fantastic shapes over fences, sheds, and dwellings. Windows were closed by drifts, and in many houses the twilight gloom was almost painful.

"Street navigation was absolutely out of the question. The sidewalks, particularly on the north side of the streets, were buried many feet deep in the snow. Pedestrians picked their way over and around drifts, blinded by the driving storm. Business was virtually suspended.

"One could only look on in wonder and amazement. All day Monday the storm continued and night shut down upon a town buried in snow. Around blazing fires we talked of the day while outside the snow piled higher and higher.

"Tuesday morning's sun rose bright and clear upon a scene of Alpine beauty. The south side of Front street was swept to the icy pavement clean as a floor but on the north side huge drifts were piled against every obstruction, awning high, and stretched out across to the opposite pavement.

"The Bay Shore street, and all around Hannah, Lay and Company's building, the drifts covered everything from five to fifteen feet deep. Cars upon the track were nearly buried from sight, doors and windows were closed tight by the huge drifts, lumber piles were covered, and roads and fences obliterated. All through the town great piles upon piles of whitest snow were packed and hammered down with sledge hammer blows from the hand of old Boreas, and stretching from walk to walk and from house to house.

"It was indeed a rare and beautiful spectacle, and will long be remembered as 'the great storm of 1881.' "

115

"Fife Lake, Michigan, January 26, 1882.

"We learn the particulars of a very sad accident which occurred on Saturday resulting in the death of two persons, Charles Bence, age 12 years, and his brother, William Bence.

"Charles left his home to go to the post office in North Fife Lake to get the mail for a number of neighbors who paid him for doing so. While on the way he met his brother, William, who was driving team for Holbrook and Carse, going to Fish Bros' Mill with a load of logs, William asked his brother to get on the load and ride over to the mill. As soon as he had unloaded, he was going to North Town and Charles could ride with him. On their arrival at the mill the logs were unloaded and William turned the team around and started them at a lively gait toward the railroad crossing, and it is said Charley told his brother it was almost mail time and they might get hurt if they attempted to cross.

"Nearly the whole way from the mill to the crossing track is shut off from view by tramways and lumber piles, while within fifty feet of the track on the south side of the wagon road a warehouse has been built right where there is a sharp curve in the railroad.

"As they emerged from behind the warehouse going at a rapid rate of speed, the train was upon them with so little warning that it was impossible to stop. The engine struck them just between the forward bob and the horses. One horse was instantly killed and the other so badly injured that it had to be shot.

"Charles was picked up and carried to a house close by, a mangled mass of humanity, his face and head bruised out of all recognition, one leg bruised and cut and the other broken above the knee and from where it was broken to the foot, mashed to a jelly. He died on Saturday night a 11:00 o'clock.

"William had five ribs crushed into his lungs and he died at 1:00 o'clock on Monday morning.

"An inquest was held by Justice Monteith and a verdict rendered in accordance with the above facts."

A Family Bewitched

"Greenville, March 15, 1883.

"Jesse Miller, a farmer living in Greenville township, Somerset county, is ready to swear that his household is afflicted with a witch. Some time ago he found a saddle hanging by the chimney. He had placed it on the balusters.

"This occurred three times, and every member of the family accused solemnly declared that they had not touched the saddle. Miller took it to the woodshed and again it was displaced. He then removed the saddle to a sawmill and spiked it to a standard. It stayed there.

"His wife was washing one day and stepped out of the apartment for a few minutes. Returning, she was amazed to find the articles which she had left in the tub thrown about over the floor.

"Miller was aroused one night by terrible screams in his front yard. He bounded out of bed and rushed out and found his daughter there alone. She had no knowledge of how she got there. Twice since she has been spirited out of the house in broad daylight in the presence of her mother and others. The spirit of darkness that exerts this influence over the young lady is invisible to all others. She describes the witch as resembling an old woman, with hoary locks, hairy face, and wearing a white cap.

"The Miller family is thoroughly terrified, as is also the entire community. Miller intends to leave the locality as soon as possible. Meanwhile, he has been in Meyersdale in quest of a witch doctor to make the place tolerable for a short time yet at least. He is firm in his witch belief."

"Genleman Thief

"Grand Rapids, Michigan, July 23, 1885.

"There is an epidemic of burglary through the southern

part of the state, especially in larger towns and cities. The species of robber who plays the leading part is dubbed 'the gentleman burglar.' His pleasant way consists in waking up the gentleman and lady of the house and while he points a revolver at their heads, begs them not to be alarmed but at the same time quietly and politely insists on the production of their watches, jewelry, silverware, and spare cash.

"To the entreaties of a Grand Rapids lady that he should not waken and alarm the children, the thief answered 'Oh no! Bless your heart, I love little children.'

"With all his politeness, the gentleman burglar is an ugly customer, and his room is better than his company.

"Murderer Shot

"Keene, N. H., July 23, 1885.

"An immense elephant belonging to Barnum's show killed his keeper last Saturday while on exhibition in New Hampshire. On Monday, at the close of a performance at Keene, it was announced that as the elephant had taken human life, he must die and volunteers were called for from the members of a local military company to shoot him. Thirty-three responded and the doomed elephant and his executioners, with thousands of spectators, took their way to a ravine a short distance from the town. The elephant was securely chained, a chalk circle marked over his heart, the command given to fire, and he died with scarcely a struggle. He was next in size to Jumbo and was valued at $10,000."

"Birds Killed by Arc Globes

"Chicago, Illinois, May 13, 1886.

"A strange phenomenon occurred during the storm Sunday night in the vicinity of the Board of Trade Electric Light at Chicago. When the watchman made his rounds, he found the sidewalks and streets in front of the tower covered with dead birds of all kinds. A little later the electrician came down and said that the great pile of birds was caused by their coming in contact with the electric light at the top of the tower.

"When he went up to the lanterns with several members of the Board of Trade, the roof was found to be covered with dead birds and each of the lamps in the big circle of light was filled with them, one globe having eight birds in it.

"These birds are of every known variety and many unfamiliar species are among them; all shades and colors are there, scarlet, blue, pink, red, canary, and matted black and white; there were some plovers among them.

"The theory is that they were migratory flocks going from south to north and were attracted by the great light, which the moment they touched, killed them. The birds are all small.

"There was a countless number of them, enough to trim all the ladies' hats in Illinois."

"New Queen of Gypsies

"Evansville, Indiana, January 20, 1887.

"The position of queen of the gypsies in the United States, made vacant by the death of Mrs. Emma Stanley which occurred near Jackson, Mississippi on December 30, has been filled by the appointment of Miss Lucy Stanley, a sister of the dead queen who lives about two miles west of Evansville, Indiana where she owns valuable property.

"Miss Stanley has gone to Dayton, Ohio to attend the funeral of the deceased queen, after which ceremony the coronation of the new queen will take place.

"Miss Stanley will remain at the place until the return of the different bands that are now in the south, when a grand jubilee will take place. After these ceremonies, which will continue for four days, have been brought to an end and her orders issued which will govern the action of this predatory people for a year, Miss Stanley will return to Evansville.

"The new queen is but 19 years old, prepossessing in appearance, fairly educated, and is a favorite not only with her own people but with all who know her. She will issue her mandates from Evansville, but will lead the annual migration of her people to the south, which commences early in November."

"Mystery Rainfall

"Augusta, Georgia, June 23, 1887.

"At Augusta, Georgia, on a space about two feet square in front of the house of John Phillips on Forsyth street, a phenomenon of nature has been occurring which has aroused the entire city and set the superstitious Negroes in the locality fairly wild with excitement.

"On Thursday night, when the sky was perfectly clear, a neighbor of Mr. Phillips noticed some very fine rain drops falling on the spot. When a sheet of paper was placed on the ground, the patter of the rain could be distinctly heard.

"The spray, coming from a continued clear sky, fell during the entire night and the following morning, even after the sun's rays fell upon it. After noon, however, it ceased, oddly to resume again at nightfall. It continued throughout that night and the next day went through the same performance. A large crowd of people is constantly attracted to the spot.

"Horrible Drought

"Henry County, Illinois, July 7, 1887.

"No such drought as now prevails had existed in Illinois and Wisconsin for many years. The roads are ankle deep with dust, the pastures are blown, and the leaves on forest and shade trees are shriveled up, and each hot breath of air from the cloudless horizon drives them away in showers.

"Creeks have run dry, and the water in the larger streams is at a lower stage than was ever known before. There has not been a soaking rain in this part of th country since March.

"The drought has become so terrible that public prayers are being offered for rain.

"The fences along country roads and the walls of the village buildings are plastered with huge bills calling for special services at the district school houses and churches.

"Fires are burning in the woods, and pastures for miles are scorched. The farmers have lost many cattle in these fires which seem to spring up in a dozen places at once. Reports from all parts of Henry and adjoining counties tell of intense suffering from the drought.

"The drinking water in many towns has been polluted, and the white beds of the creeks are covered with decaying fish. The drought in the northern and central tiers of counties of Illinois is not any more serious than it is in Wisconsin. The Badger State is literally burning up, and fruit and crops are nearly destroyed. Reports from northwestern Iowa state that the drought has been broken."

"The Champlain

"Milwaukee, Wisconsin, November 10, 1887.

"The rebuilding of the burned steamer Champlain at Milwaukee is nearly completed. Practically a new boat has been constructed. Of the Champlain only the stern post and a few feet of the keel remain. Her dimensions are as follows: Length of keel, 176 feet; over all, 180 feet; beam, 29 feet; hold, 12 feet, 6 inches.

"In constructing the hull, the model of the Champlain was preserved as nearly as possible, thus assuring speed, excellent sea-going qualities, and unusual strength. The new steamer will carry the engine of the Champlain, the working portion of which have been thoroughly overhauled under the direction of engineer McCaffrey, late of the Champlain; also the boiler, the interior having been renewed at a cost of $3,000. Like the Champlain, the steamer will have a full length cabin provided with first-class accommodations for passengers. No name has yet been chosen for the craft, but it is pretty well understood that she will be the City of Charlevoix. Captain Bishop, who was

121

mate of the Champlain, will probably command the new boat when she goes into commission as he has had charge of her construction."

"Unusual Occupation

"Springfield, Missouri, January 10, 1889.

"Mrs. Mary Hall, a middle-aged lady of Pasadena, California, who passed through the city the other night, has probably the most singular calling of any person in America. She makes a business of accompanying the bodies of persons who die in Southern California to their homes in the east, and according to her own story has found it very lucrative.

" 'I have been at the business about two years,' said she. 'How much do I get for a trip? Generally from $3 to $5 per day, my railroad fare and traveling expenses. Now it costs double, first class express rates, to send a body from California to the Missouri river, which amounts to about $300; consequently, it is cheaper to hire me, pay my expenses, and feel sure the corpse will go through safely.' "

"Six Miles An Hour Limit

"Sault Ste. Marie, Michigan, January 28, 1898.

"The Common Council of Sault Ste. Marie has passed an ordinance prohibiting driving on the principal streets of the city faster than six miles an hour.

"The Soo Times thinks the ordinance a farce and says, 'It is violated every day in the year by every man who by any means navigates in a wheeled or 'runnered' vehicle. A second class ox team will go six miles an hour. A horse with every leg spavined and suffering in the last stages of the heaves will travel six miles an hour over a corduroy road. The average man will walk at the rate of six miles an hour — that is, when he is going to supper.

"If the council had made it ten or twelve miles an hour, there would be some sense in it. There should be some law to regulate the speed of vehicles on the principal streets but any person with sense knows that it is a preposterous idea to think of limiting the speed to six miles an hour. It would be a wonder if a funeral procession wouldn't violate such a law as that.' "

"King Otto Is Dying

"Bavaria, Germany, April 8, 1898.

"The condition of the insane King Otto of Bavaria has suddenly become worse, and it is feared that he is dying. Within the last three months he has lapsed into his old violent state and his most dangerous illusion, that is, being a stork and able to fly, has again possessed him. He smokes cigarettes immoderately and displays an inordinate appetite for candles. The windows of the palace where he is confined are built up to prevent a gleam of light, which the mad king hates."

"Fire at Slights

"Slights Siding, April 22, 1898.

"Fire broke out in the saw and planing mill owned by the Lewis estate at Slights Siding about 8:30 o'clock Saturday night and totally destroyed the plant.

"The mill was formerly owned and operated by Kelley & Covell, but it recently passed into the hands of manager John Gillis. C. A. Hammond of the First National Bank is one of the trustees of the estate and he was informed of the progress of the fire through a telephone connection with the general store at Slights.

"The lumber piled in the yard is valued at $15,000 and, during the burning of the mill, this caught several times but was as often extinguished. There were, however, 15,000 shingle bands just cut that were destroyed though not insured. The lot would have been moved today.

"The insurance upon the mills was $4,500 while the loss was $10,000.

"The last person in the mill that has any business there was the engineer, who entered just before supper Saturday night to get his coat. An Indian living near stated that at dark a person was seen to leave the premises and disappear up the hill. Tracks have been discovered which corroborated this that the fire was of incendiary origin.

"The lumber cut for the season was about completed and the mill will not be rebuilt."

"New Invention

"Traverse City, Michigan, June 3, 1898.

"A model of a submarine boat is on exhibition in the window of J. N. Martinek's jewelry store and is worthy of more than passing comment. Mr. Martinek, its inventor, is also making an effort to place his machine at the service of the government but as yet he has not been able to get the attention of the navy department.

"In this regard Mr. Crozier has the advantage of him by reason of being on the ground and thus able to explain the working of his machine in person to the authorities at Washington. Mr. Martinek says that his boat is entirely different from the seventeen boats upon which patients have so far been granted."

"Bicycle Path

"Williamsburg, Michigan, June 10, 1898.

"While the bicyclers are being sadly treated by many, it is refreshing to see the way the people of Williamsburg feel about the question. The citizens of this town and the immediate vicinity are building a bicycle path from Williamsburg to Bates, a distance of four miles. The path is evenly graded, straight and well clayed. When the work is completed to Bates, they hope to push on to Acme.

"The path is twenty feet from the main road and twenty inches wide. It is raised slightly so that water will run off readily.

"The people are doing it simply for the good of the cyclists. One farmer who was working on the job said, 'We like to see 'em go by, and we want 'em to go a whizzin.'

"Such enterprise as this is surely deserving of great praise, and the bicyclers of Williamsburg, who are leading in the work, are giving a lesson to city riders that might be well taken."

"New Courthouse

"Traverse City, Michigan, June 17, 1898.

"The plans and specifications for the proposed new courthouse building are out and from the very hasty examination we have been able to give them, we have to acknowledge great disappointment at what we find.

"In our opinion, judging from these specifications, the man who is the author of them is most emphatically a 'back number.' A man who would build an ordinary courthouse with no more regard for its ventilation than is provided in this courthouse would be set down as an ignoramus so far as knowing how to plan and construct a public building is concerned.

"The building is absolutely without ventilation, except what may be had from the primitive plan of opening the windows. In this respect it is even worse than the old style of architecture where no plan for ventilating was attempted for then they warmed buildings by either stoves or fireplaces which could not be done without creating ventilation to some degree. In this case the wraming is done by direct steam heat and all chance for ventilation is cut off.

"If this is the kind of building that the board of supervisors of Grand Traverse county is going to foist upon the people for a courthouse, we certainly hope, for the sake of health and good air, that the direct steam heating will be discarded and the building be warmed with stoves instead. In the latter case some ventilation would be secured by the current necessary to create a draft in the stoves.

"The construction of this building, unless greatly modified from the present specifications, would be an outrage upon a civilized community. There are many other faults that we do not care to mention at this time, but those that we have pointed out should be sufficient to condemn it."

"Letter from Alaska

"James H. Decker of Glen Haven, who is now in the gold fields, wrote this letter to his wife

" 'Dawson City, Northwest Territory, Alaska, June 22, 1898.

" 'I will write another letter and send via of St. Michael as the boat leaves down the river right away. I have written you two letters from Dawson City that went up the river to Skaguay or Dyea or the Dalton trail, and I found out today these letters won't leave by the mounted police until the 15th of next month, so I will send this one around by St. Michael. Maybe you will receive this before you do the two that go by mounted police.

" 'Provisions are not quite as high here as they have been. Sugar has sold for one dollar a pound, now worth 40¢; tea worth $1.50 a pound. Syrup is $3.00 per gallon. Prunes and peaches $1.00 per pound. Plug tobacco has sold for $8.00 per pound, now sells for $2.50 per pound. Whiskey has been $1.00 a glass, but has taken a drop to 50¢ a drink.

" 'This is the biggest mining camp in the world. You can walk up town and see fifteen tons of gold in one pile, and a mounted policeman with a Winchester rifle loaded to the muzzle walking back and forth in front of the boodle all of the time.

" 'There are two other places like that. The McDonalds fetched in a pack train loaded with gold. That means seven or eight mules. Four men were on the trail with all they could carry and a man walking behind with a repeater and armed to the teeth.

" 'I will mail this letter and hoist sail for Eagle City, you can see by the map where it is. It is called Forty Mile there. I will build another boat, a river boat smaller than the first one, and go up Forty Mile river one hundred and twenty-five miles

126

to what is called the new gold field of Alaska. It is in God's country, in Uncle Sam's territory.

" 'From there we can reach Seventy Mile river or cross the mountains and strike the head waters of the Copper river. It may take six months for a letter to reach you, but I am determined to not show my face until I find gold. It is very hot here and we travel at night, but there is no night here. Give my best regard to my friends and tell them they will never know what hardships are until they strike Klondyke country. But I am determined not to be weakened as long as my health lasts. I am feeling good and in the best of spirits. Billy and Levi Iles are well and full of hope.

James H. Decker' "

"Mrs. Carrie Nation on Warpath
"Anthony, Kansas, January 31, 1901.

"Twelve women of the W.C.T.U. armed with pickaxes, hatchets, and hammers yesterday raided and completely demolished four saloons, known as 'joints'.

"During the early hours of the morning, before many citizens had reached their places, 12 members of the local branch of the W.C.T.U. marched quietly down the principal street of the town. They carried a miscellaneous collection of axes, hatchets, etc. Several of the women were accompanied by their husbands, who, however, took no part in the proceedings and acted only as a sort of bodyguard.

"It was observed by those on the streets that the party was headed for a so-called joint, and a good sized crowd soon collected.

"In the rear of a drug store was situated the first point of attack. Entrance was effected through a back door. The place contained costly bar fixtures and quite a stock of liquors. The fixtures and cash register were demolished, but the bulk of the liquor was stored out of sight and escaped destruction.

"Half a block further on, the second scene of the crusade was enacted. The door was locked, but entrance was quickly made with an axe. While part of the women gave their attention to the door, others reduced the plate glass front to powder. Back of the bar was a heavy plate mirror. This, as well as everything else, was destroyed.

"The proprietor of the place entered when the smashing process was at its height. He attempted to stop the work, but came into collision with a husband-bodyguard. A blow on the head with a beer bottle quickly rendered the irate proprietor helpless, blood from a deep cut in his scalp mixing with liquor which flowed in streams over the floor.

"Two more 'joints' were visited in quick succession. Their furniture was demolished and the stocks of liquor were emptied into the gutters.

"Complete as the work of destruction apparently had been, it was stated that plenty of the prohibited liquids had been stored away in safe places in anticipation of just such raids. The 'jointists' were chiefly concerned over the destruction of their fixtures valued at several thousands of dollars.

"After the work of demolition was completed, the crusaders held a prayer meeting on the sidewalk and 'Nearer My God to Thee' was sung with great fervor.

"Mrs. Sheriff of Danville, a village near by, was the leader in yesterday's raid. She came to Anthony Tuesday night, quietly organized the local temperance women, and planned the crusade. Several members of the band were mere schoolgirls, who, however, took a leading part in the work. Mrs. Sheriff, the leader, previously had destroyed the fixtures at a saloon at Danville, and is credited, locally, with having given Mrs. Nation her first idea for a wrecking crusade."

"Topeka, Kansas, January 3, 1901.

"The Kansas State Temperance Union, which is holding its annual convention here, subscribed over $100 to purchase a gold medal for Mrs. Carrie Nation. Mrs. Hutchinson, president of the state W.C.T.U., was made chairman of a committee to design and purchase the medal. The fund was started by Col. C. B. Cook who donated $10 'to help purchase a gold medal for the bravest woman in Kansas, Mrs. Nation.'

"When Mrs. Nation heard what had been done, she cried a little, and then scolded those who had planned the surprise.

"She said she would take the money and turn it over to the fund to aid her work, but she would have no medal. Mrs. Nation said she would remain in Topeka until every one of the 120 saloons are closed."

"Topeka, Kansas, February 1, 1901.

"With a mob of 500 people following her, Mrs. Carrie Nation visited seven Topeka saloons this morning and warned the proprietors that she would return next week and demolish the places. She was followed by two policemen who had orders to see that she was not molested either by the mob or the saloon keepers. At each place she was stopped by guards who warned her not to attempt to do any damage."

"Northport
"Northport, Michigan, February 15, 1901.

"From time to time there has been mention of the new resort, Northport Point, and what is to be done there the coming season. The whole changes contemplated are thus summarized by the Northport Leader:

" 'Northport people will be interested to know that a great many improvements will be made this spring at Northport Point resort. Mr. Fred Giddings, who managed the hotel last season, has purchased it and will make a great many changes in and around the place, all conducive to the comfort and convenience of the guests. He will add 60 feet on the north end of Cedar Lodge and carry it up three stories in height and add sleeping rooms to accommodate one hundred guests. He will put in a wind engine, tower, and big reservoir for supplying the hotel with a complete waterworks system, build a complete sewage system, and add many other little conveniences,

"Kehl Bros. will erect a pagoda or pavilion on the dock over there and supply it with the many articles which the tourists want so much to purchase such as Indian work, confectionary, etc., and will have some competent person to take charge of it.

"A boat will be put on to run on schedule time between the Point and Northport for the accommodation of the summer visitors and the Northport people who wish to go back and forth on business or pleasure. This will be a great convenience.

"Mr. O. A. Ward will build one modern cottage and possibly more. Mr. Winans of Kalamazoo also has plans drawn for a new cottage which he will begin work on as soon as the weather will permit Joseph Kehl will also build a cottage on his lot over there which he purchased last year. A number of others are figuring on plans for cottages that will either be built this spring or fall. A lot of new sidewalk around the Point is another improvement that is being planned.

"Last year was the first year of Northport Point resort history and was crowded to overflowing. Accommodations could not be supplied to all who came and a number had to tent out on account of lack of sleeping apartments while a number were sent away. Mr. Giddings will soon be here to make arrangements for building and just as soon as spring opens, the hustle and bustle of business will prove the assertion that we have already made that Northport is on the eve of a reawakening and on the eve of an era of prosperity.' "

"New Brewery
"Traverse City, Michigan, February 22, 1901.

"Joseph Gambs, proprietor of the new brewery for Traverse City, is in the city and let the contract Wednesday for the new building to the Huetteman & Cramer Co. of Detroit.

"H. C. Wiedman, general manager and secretary of the company, is in the city and already has a force of men engaged hauling stone to their location on East Front street.

"The Huetteman & Cramer Co. are manufacturers of brewers, brickmakers, and refrigerating machinery and also furnish complete outfits for breweries. The superintendent for the new works will arrive in a few days, when the plant will be pushed to completion as rapidly as possible.

"The new building will be of brick, furnished from the yard of J. W. Markham, and will be three stories high. The interior will be constructed of steel with asphalt with cement floors, making the cellars entirely without wood. The building will be completely modern in its construction, equipped with the latest improved machinery and refrigerating apparatus.

"The size of the brew house will be 37x42 feet; the wash house, 30x18; the racking room, 30x18; and the cellars, 37x40. The plant will be one of the most modern in the country with a capacity of 12,000 to 15,000 barrels per year built at a cost of over $46,000. The capacity of the plant may be increased to 20,000 barrels without altering the building.

"Mr. Gambs will have charge of the plant himself, as he is a thorough and practical brewer, having been brewmaster for Pabst in Milwaukee for a number of years. He was also connected with the Muskegon Brewery and for fifteen years was associated with the Manistee Brewery. He will build a home here and make Traverse City his permanent location.

"It was through the instrumentality of Fred C. Toele of Detroit, promoter of breweries, that Traverse City secured the new enterprise as he is in touch with all the openings in the country.

"Mr. Gambs states that, weather permitting, the plant will have goods on the market in July. There is no reason why Traverse City is not the best location that he could have found, for from its central location he can reach his trade in the northern part of the state very easily.

"Lather & Smith have been awarded the contract for building the new ice house for the brewery. Work will be commenced Monday."

"Will Open A Hospital

"Traverse City, Michigan, June 7, 1901.

"The city is to have that long contemplated hospital. It will not, however, be built by the city nor yet be under the auspices of the Woman's Club, as has been contemplated at one time and another.

"The projectors of the new and much needed institution are Drs. Garner and Swanton. The purchase of the residence at 602 Washington street, corner Franklin, has been made by them, from James Dunn, and the house is now being fitted up for occupancy which it is expected will occur by the first of next week.

"The new hospital will be made to accommodate between ten and fifteen patients at a time and it is the intention of the physicians to keep a competent corps of nurses and have everything modern and up-to-date in the way of conveniences and furnishings.

"The hospital will fill a long needed want in the city and already the physicians, who are to be its managers, have received applications for room and have one operation scheduled to occur upon the opening of the institution next week."

"Fourth of July Accidents

"Traverse City, Michigan, July 12, 1901.

"There came within an ace of being a fatal Fourth of July accident when Roby Gibbs, the 11 year old son of H. E. Gibbs, picked up a giant firecracker which had burned down the fuse and remarked there was a very large hole in the explosive, then dropped it to the ground. The cracker had scarcely left his hands when it exploded. It was then so near to him that his left hand was badly shattered by the concussion. Two large gashes, one across the left hand and the other at the base of the thumb, were cut deep into the flesh. The accident happened at Bassett Island where a party had gone in Mr. Gibb's launch. The launch had scarcely more than touched the shore before the lad was out,

132

the firecracker lighted, and the accident over with. The boy was brought home in the launch and Dr. Garner dressed his wound.

"Another little boy nearly lost an eye and it will take a day or two yet to tell whether the sight can be saved. Bennie Robertson, Alex Robertson's little son, went with his parents up the river to the power house. In the afternoon the lad was struck in the left eye by exploding powder and the eye badly injured. He was conveyed to Dr. Martin's office and the powder removed. The eye is yet so badly swollen it will take a few days to determine whether the sight is there or not.

"George Harrison was showing some of the boys out on Lake avenue how it was done and badly burned the inside of his hands.

" 'Cy' Hall, Lester Hall's little boy, and Frank Daniels, Malcolm Winnie's step-son, had their faces badly burned by powder. Dr. Anderson patched both boys up."

"A Golden Crucifix
"Frankfort, Michigan, July 12, 1901.

"Great excitement prevails here over the finding of the golden altar crucifix by workmen at the new Ann Arbor Hotel. The crucifix, which is eleven inches in length, the cross five inches long at arms, is mounted on a base two inches square, heavily plated with gold and was undoubtedly the property of Father Marquette, buried here 225 years ago.

"The finding of a skull on the same spot some time ago caused great excitement and this proves without a doubt that the celebrated explorer was buried here.

"History states he was buried four streams south of Little Traverse Bay, which is Betsey river which forms the harbor here. The crucifix is of French origin and bears the letters I.N.R.T. It is now in possession of the hotel contractor, Charles Hoertz, who has expressed his intention of sending it to the Kent County Historical Collection at Grand Rapids, Michigan.

"It is of priceless value as a relic and could easily be disposed of for a large sum. The Ann Arbor people are anxious to get possession of it to be placed in the hotel along with the skull as a relic and a great fight is expected over it as Hoertz refuses to give it up. It would be a great drawing card for the company."

"Advertisement

"Traverse City, Michigan, October 18, 1901.

"The Boston Specialists have located their offices at 619 Union street. These eminent specialists treat all chronic diseases and deformities of men, women, and children. The rich and the poor alike are treated. You need not bring money as consultation and advice are free. All that is asked in return for their services is that every person treated will state to their friends the result obtained by their new system. All who call upon the doctors before November 2nd will receive the benefit of their services until cured free of charge. If you have rheumatism, kidney, or bladder trouble, paralysis, heart disease, nervous debility, or constipation, come and be cured by our new system. The doctors will locate your disease without asking you any questions.

"Deafness is cured by an entirely new system. Also cancers, tumors, ulcers, and all blood, skin, and scalp diseases. They cure piles and rupture and guarantee every case as curable. If you have catarrh or lung trouble, be examined. If you are improving under your family physician, do not go and take up their valuable time. Office hours, 9 A.M. to 8 P.M."

"Improvement Organization

"Empire, Michigan, December 20, 1901.

"Through the efforts of E. R. Daily, of this village, and Smurthwaite & Foster, of this city, an organization with a capital of $10,000 has been effected called The Grand Traverse Development Company, which elected officers today. They are: George C. Wilce, president; E. R. Daily, vice-president; Thomas Smurthwaite, secretary; and W. H. Foster, treasurer.

134

"The directors are: George C. Wilce and E. R. Daily of the Empire Lumber Co.; C. D. Stanely of Suttons Bay; W. J. Foster, Thomas Smurthwaite, Mrs. Smurthwaite, and Mrs. Foster of Traverse City.

"The objects of the company as set forth in the articles are 'To bring owners of real estate in contact with parties wishing to purchase lands in their care and disposal; to act as agent for persons desiring to purchase lands; to encourage and locate manufacturing enterprises; and to perform such other services within the scope of Act. No. 207 of the laws of 1877 of the State of Michigan as will tend to the development of the so-called Grand Traverse Region.' "

Chapter VII

ERA OF THE OPERA HOUSE

The railroads were invading the Middle West and, like the roots of a giant elm, were branching off in all directions in search of nurture.

To many places the coming of the rails brought a first firm contact with the outside world; offered an opportunity to the pioneer to receive news before it became history.

Earlier, the box social, the square dance, the political speech, and the amateur "program" in the one-room school had provided the entertainment fare. Gradually it became inadequate.

The repertoire companies and the opera companies of metropolitan communities began to move with the rails, invading the remote rural areas and "tank towns" in the wilderness.

Thus was born the era of the "opera house" as a cultural achievement in the long isolated lumber towns, shipping centers, and other backwoods communities.

In Northern Michigan the Grand Traverse Region was a focal point. Pine was king. Iron was second in line, being smelted in several locations. Charcoal was being turned out by the trainload. Lumber was making millionaires.

Over a span of years during which the opera houses brought entertainment, culture, politics, social intermingling, and fun to the timber towns, there was a rapid growth in the understanding of what was going on "outside."

It was unusual that not one, but two opera houses would spring into being in Traverse City, tagged "Queen City" of the north.

The first opera house in Traverse City was constructed by Bartak, Bartak, and Wilhelm. Ground was broken on April 16,

137

1891 on the south side of the 100 block of East Front street. This was before plans for the building had been completed and, as an announcement explains on May 7, the original plans had been changed and the building would house four stores instead of an originally planned three.

Brickwork on the City Opera House started on Tuesday, July 23, 1891. The red brick for the building was shipped from Akron, Ohio. The iron roof for the building arrived on July 30 and was installed by Despries and Montague, who also installed the heating and plumbing facilities.

On December 17, 1891, an announcement was made that an informal opening of the City Opera Hall would be held Christmas night, Friday, December 25. Music was furnished by the Ideal Orchestra, a local music aggregation, and an oyster supper was served by the City Cafe which was housed in the same building.

On New Year's Eve the management scheduled a holiday ball with the Boys' Band providing dancing music.

The first play booked into the new City Opera House was "Avenged," announcement of which was made on February 4.

"Avenged" showed and the *Grand Traverse Herald*, contemporary newspaper of that day, printed the following review:

" 'Avenged' played here on Monday and was the vilest thing that ever showed in Traverse City. The proprietors of the City Opera House feel worse than anyone else about it. There was a good audience of over 600 and all were pleased with the new hall and, we believe, will not feel disposed to criticize the management. They were as badly sold as was the public."

In the meantime Julius Steinberg, who had arrived in Traverse City as a peddler carrying his stock in trade on his back, saw the handwriting on the theater backdrop.

Steinberg had prospered, and from a meager stock in trade had expanded his business until he owned a splendid clothing and dry goods store on East Front Street in Traverse City. Without declaring his intentions to build an opera house, he announced in January, 1891 that he had purchased forty-five additional feet of property and would build a brick block building in the spring.

The new Steinberg property was the site of the village fire engine house and brought his Front Street holdings to 115 feet. The old engine house was torn down to make way for the new development.

In March, 1891, Steinberg stated that the plans for his building were about completed. For the first time he hinted that the first floor would be for his business and the two upper floors would be an opera house.

The proposed opera house, which was referred to as "The Traverse City Opera House," was, for that day, to be elegant to the last degree. It was to be steam-heated and electrically lighted.

It wasn't until May, 1891, that work actually began on the new building. The first earth was turned on Tuesday morning the week of May 14, 1891.

Stone for the foundation arrived in July of that year and the walls were well on their way up in August. During September and October there was a delay in constructions. Julius Steinberg was a devout Hebrew and two long Jewish holidays brought work to a semi-halt. Even the Steinberg store closed.

In December the brickwork was completed, the scaffolding was removed from the imposing building, and Despries and Montague were given the contract for heating.

Cost of the structure was estimated at $60,000 and the opera house area included a stage 32 x 45 feet, proscenium 19 x 36 feet, eight dressing rooms, and the opera house was illuminated by 400 electric globes.

Then there was a lull in activity at the "finest opera house north of Chicago." It is assumed that a financial crisis reared its head in the Steinberg family. Until December of 1893 there was, so far as records go, complete inactivity. Late in 1894 Steinberg advertised a gigantic sale in the clothing and dry goods store which he owned. Purpose, he said, was to raise $10,000 to com-

139

plete the block, including the opera house, which was to be officially called "Steinberg's Grand Opera House."

On December 11, 1894, a grand opening show was presented at the establishment when Walker Whiteside, a leading American tragedian, portrayed Hamlet in that Shakespeare production.

The event was the finest social conclave ever held in Traverse City. The ladies wore their party prettiest and the gentlemen dressed in their Sunday best. Flowers were at a premium at the Traverse City Floral Company as the fair sex scrambled to secure corsages.

The cloak room received almost as much praise as the glittering theater. It was the first performance in Traverse City where the ladies and their escorts could check their hats and coats.

The walls of the opera house were tan, blue, and gold. The seats on the main floor were so installed as to be easily removed, converting the area into a dance floor. Music was furnished by the Ideal Orchestra, composed of local musicians.

The second performance given in Steinberg's Grand Opera House was Bulwer's great play "Richelieu," in which Whiteside again appeared.

Unlike the review of the first play in the City Opera House, the reviews of the first two shows in Steinberg's were effervescent to the last degree.

On December 29, 1894, Steinberg booked "New Dominion" which was produced by the Frohman Company and, again, the house was packed and the public was enthusiastic.

The consistently fine plays which were offered at Steinberg's Grand Opera House caused it to immediately surge ahead of the City Opera House in popularity. It was gay, colorful, and "big cityish."

About this time the City Opera House opened its stage to local thespians, talent shows, school programs, graduation ceremonies, and similar entertainment and functions.

Going back to mid-April, 1892, the Bohemian Dramatic Club staged "Bratr Honak." This humorous character play was

140

a sellout with admission set at thirty-five cents. The drama club "Cechie" presented several plays and entertainment features during the years before the turn of the century.

The dramatic department of St. Francis School had a successful show in June, 1892 . . . and so it went. Lectures, parties, weddings, variety shows, and many more events took place in the City Opera House.

In the spring of 1895 the Traverse City High School held its 20th annual commencement program in the establishment. A total of thirty-two students were to receive diplomas. Then the matter of "equal time" reared its pointed little head. It was decided, in all fairness, that Steinberg's Grand Opera House should play a part in the graduation program. Compromise was reached and the Baccalaureate was held in the Steinberg building. Leon Steinberg, son of Julius, was the valedictorian and the class oration was by Jerry Sullivan. Graduation ceremonies were held in the City Opera House.

Julius Steinberg was not one to miss an opportunity to keep his opera house on a paying basis. Many of his programs were printed eight pages with local advertising on every page. The feature was sandwiched in between the display announcements. In 1894-95 he featured local thespians in many support roles. Such names as Louis Morrison and Eugene Power appeared as members of the cast in several plays. Chief usher in those long-gone days was Charles Hale. D. F. Campbell was the chief electrician.

From 1900, through a span of 15 years, both opera houses in Traverse City prospered. There was a rivalry, sometimes not too friendly but certainly healthy, which brought theatrical entertainment of high quality to the booming north country.

Among the popular actors of the day was William S. Hart. He appeared at Steinberg's Grand Opera House and is reported to have made a classic remark while visiting with a local theatergoer. The occasion was when Hart stood at the back of the theater looking out over Boardman River and Grand Traverse Bay.

"It's wonderful," he said, "Suckers at the front door and suckers at the back door."

Around 1913, the stock companies were still touring the country. Sometimes they held one-night stands and sometimes three-night stands. The repertoire companies usually played a week. The Whitney Stock Company was one of the favorites and usually packed the house. Such plays as "Paid in Full" and "A Night in Chinatown" were among the hilarious situation comedy plays presented.

One of the most popular shows ever presented in the City Opera House or in Steinberg's Grand was "Miss Fearless and Company." It featured a cast of local people and was directed by Mrs. J. V. MacIntosh. To quote from the program, "The leading characters are all taken by well known society women who are willing to give of their time and services for the good of the cause."

Through the years that the two institutions were in their full bloom of popularity, there was no dearth of "something to do."

The minstrel shows held the spotlight on many occasions in both Traverse City opera houses.

One of these companies brings memories to a few of the senior citizens of the north. It was a minstrel group which arrived in Traverse City after a stand in Cadillac.

"The ghost hadn't walked for a couple of weeks," Harold Titus recalls. "The cast got paid in Cadillac, and they got roaring drunk on the train. The outfit got into town all plastered, and the director had to rustle up a band. The troupe always had a band to play in front of the opera house before show time to attract a crowd.

"They would tootle there a little while and then go into the theater and go into the pit where they played for the show. Well, on this occasion they called us, the local group, backstage and the musical director gave us the cues and we got out there and were doing a job for them. Fred Harig was playing clarinet

142

this night and he was sitting next to me on my left. I played, as I said, the flute.

"They had the chaps who were plastered stretched out along the partition and, at the time of which I speak, one of the cast was singing a bass solo. Fred was playing an obligatto. The boys were doing pretty well with 'Asleep in the Deep' when one of the drunks rolled over and kicked the partition. Fred laughed into his clarinet and the thing squealed and we darn near broke up the show."

Some of the itinerant shows arrived with an entire carload of scenery and their own stage hands. So familiar were the men with their work that they could set up a stage in an hour.

Later the bulky scenery was replaced with what they called "Diamond Dye" scenery. The scenes were painted on drop curtains with Diamond Dye and were less cumbersome. For a change of scenery all that was necessary was to unroll a back-drop and there it was.

As time moved inexorably along, there came serious competition to the opera houses and the shows which made regular visits to the growing communities. The moving picture was on its way in. Where the stage show charged ten cents, twenty-five cents, fifty cents, and sometimes more, the movie houses were bringing entertainment for as little as five cents an admission.

Business waned for the grand old institution of the opera house. Attendance fell off and many of the acting and entertainment companies turned to the "tent show," which involved a three-night stand in small communities where there had been, heretofore, no facilities for stage shows.

"Uncle Tom's Cabin," "Peck's Bad Boy," "East Lynn," and a score of other such plays continued to make their rounds for many years, drawing goodly attendance and being received with much acclaim.

Then it came to an end. The tent show was no more and the opera houses closed their doors.

Steinberg's beautiful place of entertainment was dismantled.

Some of the seats were used in a moving picture theater and much of the interior was remodeled to accommodate business.

The City Opera House was also closed but it was never dismantled. The old backdrop with its colorful advertising, dust-covered and web-strewn, still hangs. The private theater boxes are still in place and the seats, most of them, are still as they were in another era. Only ghosts of old memories walk the ramp and stand before the footlights.

To some of those who remember, the City Opera House and Steinberg's Grand Opera House are as the pages of a wonderful book, read and closed, but haunting in its frequent retelling.

Chapter VIII

WAS MOTHER A GOOD COOK?

Was mother's cooking better than what is being prepared in the kitchens of today? It is an argument that no amount of discussion will settle. The younger generation of housewives will bring up the old rebuttal about vitamins, and calories, balanced diet, proteins, fats, etc. They will point with pride to a pretty table and remind you that grandmother's table never looked so nice.

Before we can conduct an intelligent discussion about the quality of grandmother's cooking we should first realize that there were no electric mixers or frying pans. There were no automatic percolators or toasters, nor did grandmother have an electric- or gas-operated refrigerator or stove. There was no giant deep freeze in the basement, nor was there an eighty-gallon water heater.

Grandmother never dreamed of going to the corner store to buy a box of ready-mix cake which would require only the addition of a bit of milk to prepare it for the oven. Nor, could she buy a beef stew in a can, an apple pie ready to bake. In fact, grandmother was so old-fashioned she had never heard of a pizza pie.

Equipment which was common in all pioneer kitchens included a kneadboard, a mixing bowl, a rolling pin, and a sprawling kitchen range. In the old cabinet there was a flour bin and in the cupboard was a box of saleratus ("bicarb" to you members of the ulcer club) and a can of popular brand baking soda. Of course there was a wide variety of spices because spices and herbs were kitchen necessities in those days.

For bread baking there was usually a crock of "starter"; a yeast which was carried over from baking to baking because

147

yeast cakes weren't always available. Sometimes the pioneer housewife made her own yeast, using cornmeal, potatoes, etc.

"There ain't no cookin' like what was done on the old cook stove," oldtimers will tell you. But it is admitted that, with its complication of drafts and dampers, its warming closet and its reservoir for hot water, it turned out a pretty tasty meal.

With all of this discussion about old-fashioned cooking comes a desire to know what some of the old tried-and-true recipes were like. In making a study of the old recipes it will be noted that there were no minute details. The ingredients in their amounts were given and any housewife was supposed to have enough God-given sense to put the stuff together.

Mrs. J. W. Dickerman, who lived at the Solon Station in 1885, listed a recipe for "poor man's cake" as being her favorite. Here is how it went:

"One cup sour cream, one cup sugar, two cups of flour, two eggs, one teaspoon soda, flavor."

That was it! From that point you were on your own. Sequence of ingredients, how long to bake, or how large the cake, was something you were supposed to know.

A pioneer recipe for corn starch cake was written by Mrs. W. W. Burton of Leland, Michigan. This is how it was made:

"One cup of sugar, one-half cup of butter, one-half cup of sweet milk, one cup of flour, one-half cup of corn starch, two eggs, one teaspoon cream of tartar, and one-half teaspoon soda."

French toast, as we know it today, was not served. Late in the last century Mrs. C. O. Titus of Traverse City, Michigan suggested a delicious way (circa 1880) to prepare this breakfast treat. Simply take a slice of bread, toast it and dip it in warm, salted water. Place it in a dish, sprinkle it with sugar and cinnamon and serve hot.

In the wilderness country, salt pork was, more often than not, the main meat course for a family meal. A housewife would throw up her hands in holy horror if she were asked to serve "baked salt pork" today.

But, in the days of the pine it was a common supper food. It was prepared by soaking a piece of salt pork in sweet milk overnight. This was to remove some of the salt. Then the top of the pork was scored with a sharp knife, marking it deeply in half-inch squares. Then the scoring was filled with regular dressing made from bread crumbs, sage and moistened with some of the milk in which the meat was soaked. It was baked in a hot oven, and basted with the drippings.

Then, there was pork fricassee, pork potpie, stuffed pork, and pork pie with onions and tomato.

Cold salt pork was also served. The meat was sliced, dipped in a batter of beaten eggs, then in cracker meal and fried. Today it would be considered somewhat repulsive.

Of course, cornbread and johnny cake were common in the pioneer kitchen. There was a difference between the two. One was a raised loaf and the other was a pan-baked flatbread. The art of making cornbread, or Indian bread, as it ws sometimes called, is gone. Not even bakeries attempt to imitate it. Cornbread was a heavy, flavorful bread using corn meal about four parts to one part flour. The texture was fine to a point of being soggy. Our grandparents thought it was delicious.

Dried fruits, molasses, beans, and dairy and poultry products were the staff of life in the pioneer home. Almost every family had a small flock of chickens and each family supported a cow, or vice versa.

One thing we must remember, in discussing the table fare of a past generation: There was always a hearty appetite at meal time. Work in the woods, the mills, on the farms, was hard work. There were no eight-hour days or forty-hour weeks. It was work from sun up until sun down. Folks got hungry.

Perhaps it is the memories of those appetites which have helped glorify the cooking of the pioneer housewife.

A modern housewife, asked how she would prepare salt pork to serve to unexpected guests, replied "I wouldn't." Another young housewife, asked how she would go about making bean dumplings, shrugged her shoulders and said "They sound terrible."

Dumplings, light or soggy, were common fare fifty years ago. There were bean dumplings, potato dumplings, tomato dumplings, chicken dumplings, beef broth and dumplings and, of course, the always popular, but baked, apple dumplings.

Potatoes were prepared in many different ways. Mother prepared "milk potatoes" which were first cousin to the more fine-sounding and modern scalloped potatoes. Raw fried potatoes, crispy brown from an iron skillet (if you lived in Michigan, or a "spider" if you were a Hoosier) were always popular. Raw fries, pancakes, and golden brown fried salt pork, topped with a piece of apple pie (probably dried apples) was a breakfast fit for a robust appetite.

Pancakes of a few generations ago were not the works of art served in today's home. For instance, there were buckwheat cakes, made with a thin batter and baked on a "three-cake" griddle. The housewife used a good portion of "drippings" on the griddle to insure each cake a crisp ring around its outside.

Not many people today will remember sour dough pancakes. One housewife in northern Michigan boasted that she hadn't changed her dough crock for three years. Any family with a tooth for sour dough cakes could be spotted across a forty-acre field. There was an odor about a dough crock that has never been duplicated by man or nature. But the cakes, with their tart flavor, were good . . . awfully good.

Baked goods, today, are considered stale if twenty-four hours old. Grandmother would bake once a week and the big brown loaves of bread were just as tasty a week later although a little short on moisture.

Friedcakes were good twice; once while they were fresh from the tallow kettle and again when they were two or three days old. When they were fried in tallow or "half and half," they were usually placed on a cookie tin and warmed in the oven. Otherwise they coated the roof of the mouth with tallow . . . a sensation hard to describe.

150

Sometimes, when mother was baking bread, she would set aside a small portion of the dough and, by adding a bit of sugar, create delicious "buns." They weren't the delicate, fluffy bits with which we moderns are afflicted. They were firm and flavorful and, we like to believe, nourishing.

Naturally, the cellar was a backstop on the occasion of unexpected guests. In addition to the hundreds of quarts of fruit and pickles therein, mother liked to "fry down" some sausage and store it in gallon crocks. Sorghum molasses in gallon crocks was also an old stand-by. It tasted like twentieth century stock food.

Head cheese and liver sausage, salvage products from butchering time, were always stored in the cellar in crocks and sliced out to be served cold or warmed up.

The old kitchen range had its good points, despite the chore of splitting wood, filling the reservoir, taking out the ashes and, about twice a year — "blacking."

Left-over food could always be stored in the warming closet where the stove pipe provided constant heat. Then, on the back of the range, say over the third griddle, there was often a pot of "soup stock" simmering. Any person in his right mind will admit that beef-vegetable soup isn't good until it has cooked about two — maybe three days. The old kettle, sometimes cast iron, contained a few pieces of "rib meat" and a lot of vegetables. Seasoned with salt and pepper . . . its goodness can't be described.

Baked potatoes have lost their appeal. In the modern home today they are served very prettily. They come split open, with a patty of butter in the center, or a dab of sour cream which tastes like rancid library paste, and a sprig or two of parsley at the proper angle. Sometimes the potato is wrapped in shiny foil — a mark of a modern housewife and an abomination to Aunt Sarah.

But what has happened to the baked potato which was served in the round, cut up skin and all, covered with sausage gravy, from which mother forgot to remove all of the sausage,

151

and eaten with a thick slice of bread and butter. Imagine eating the skin of a potato! Shade of Duncan Hines.

Incidentally, an old recipe book of 1885 states that not one housewife in ten knows how to boil potatoes. Here are the recommendations: Leave the skins on, bring water to a boil and "throw" the potatoes in the pot. When they are soft, put them in cold water immediately. Leave in cold water two minutes and drain. Now put them back in the empty pot and place them on the back of the range with the cover half removed until the skins are dry. Peel and serve in an open dish, never a covered dish.

Of course there was "fancy cookin' " in the pioneer days. There were cakes and cookies, currant fritters, and all kinds of tarts. There were cream fritters, whipped syllabub, and Spanish custard.

The list could reach from here to society and back. There was dandy Jack, nonpareil, cucumber catsup, spiced plums, frogs with tomatoes, baked chicken with parsnips, and lemon snaps.

And, from all of that came the modern cook who can whip up a delicious meal in nothing flat. She can accept unexpected company with the nonchalance of a pioneer and when supper time (now it's dinner) rolls around, she can say "grace" (grandma returned "thanks") over a delicious and appetizing meal . . . like at the Stork Club. Providing, of course, she can find her can opener.

Chapter IX

RECIPES OF YESTERYEAR

"Ginger Ale

"Ginger ale is the foundation of many agreeable drinks and punches, since almost all fruits and flavors seem to harmonize well with the ginger and lemon of which it is made.

"In two gallons of water dissolve three pounds of granulated sugar, and add the beaten whites of three eggs and two ounces of ground ginger, previously dissolved in water. Let the mixture come to a boil, skim and set aside to cool. Now add the juice of four large lemons, one-fourth a yeast cake (compressed) previously dissolved in little water, and stir the mixture thoroughly.

"Let stand for a few minutes, and then strain through a cheesecloth bag, and pour into bottles. Set away in a cool dark place, and in forty-eight hours the ginger ale will be ready to drink. An acid flavor may be given to this ale by squeezing the juice of half a lemon into a tumbler and then filling the glass with the ale."

"Quince Preserves

"Wash and wipe the quinces. Pare, core, and cut into slices, or they may be quartered. Be sure to throw each piece into cold water to prevent discoloration. Put them into the kettle and barely cover with boiling water. Simmer until tender; skim out the fruit very carefully and add the parings but not the cores to the liquid; cover and simmer one hour. Strain and to every pint of this juice allow one pint of sugar; stir until dissolved.

"Bring quickly to the boiling point and boil hard (if there is a quart of juice) fifteen minutes. Skim well. Now put in the quinces and boil until clear and red. It is better to keep them covered if you wish them bright in color.

"When the quinces are done, skim out into hot jelly glasses. Boil the juice, if necessary, a little longer to become thick; pour this over the fruit and stand in the sunshine to finish and seal."

"Sweetbread Salad

"Two pairs of sweetbreads dropped in boiling salt water and cooked from 20 to 30 minutes, then plunged in very cold water for a few minutes.

"Take equal quantity of celery and one tablespoonful of chopped almonds. In cucumber season, use them in place of the celery; it is fine."

"Sea Foam

"Cook two cups of light brown sugar, with enough water to cover it, until it will form a soft ball when dropped into cold water; then add two well beaten whites of eggs and beat constantly until it thickens.

"Drop with a spoon upon greased paper and put half of an English walnut on each piece and let stand until it hardens."

"Transparent Pie

"One cup of butter, one cup of brown sugar, yolks of three eggs, all well beaten together. Bake with one crust."

"Suet Pudding

"One-half cup of sugar, one cup of molasses, one cup sour milk, one cup suet, one cup raisins, three cups of flour, one-half teaspoonful of soda and salt, one nutmeg, and cinnamon. Steam for three hours and serve with dip."

"Vanilla and Lemon Ice Cream

"To make a gallon freezer full, take two and a half quarts of cream, 18 ounces of granulated sugar, three eggs well beaten and one tablespoonful of vanilla extract. Freeze until stiff. To make lemon ice cream add one tablespoonful of lemon extract to a gallon of vanilla ice cream."

"Dandelion Wine

"One full quart of dandelion blooms, one gallon water, one lemon cut in slices (not peeled), and two and a half pounds of sugar. Put in a kettle and boil five minutes, then pour into a jar; when cold, add two tablespoonfuls of good yeast. Keep in a warm place three days until it ferments, then strain and bottle. Cork tightly."

"Elder Blossom Wine

"Add one gallon boiling water to one quart of elder blossoms and let stand one hour; then strain and add three pounds of sugar. Boil a little and skim.

"Let stand until lukewarm; then add one lemon, sliced fine, and one tablespoonful good yeast. Let stand 24 hours. Strain and put into bottles or jugs, filling full until all impurities are worked out. Be sure to fill up jugs as fast as it works out, and the wine will be a beautiful amber color.

"In making this wine, great care should be taken to keep all stems out, as they make the wine taste rank and give it a dark color."

"Blackberry Wine

"First measure the berries and bruise them; add one quart of boiling water to each gallon; let the mixture stand 24 hours, stirring occasionally. Strain off the liquor and put into a cask; to every gallon add two pounds of sugar; cork tight and let stand till the next October, when it will be ready for use. It may be bottled if desired."

"Pear Chips

"Ten pounds of pears sliced thin, seven pounds of sugar and four lemons boiled soft. Press out the juice and pulp, then chop the peel very fine.

157

"Boil the sugar and fruit together until soft; then add the lemon, one-half pound green ginger root scraped and cut into bits. Let all boil slowly until quite thick. Can be put in jelly glasses and sealed with paper."

"Breaded Ham

"Cut one pound of ham in slices one-fourth inch thick; lay in hot water for 30 minutes, drain and wipe dry, dip in beaten egg, then in rolled bread crumbs and broil."

"Chicken and Macaroni

"In a baking pan arrange layers of bits of chicken, macaroni and bread crumbs, the crumbs on top. Season with salt, pepper, and butter. Pour over a dressing made of two cups of stock, one-half cup of cream. Add flour to thicken. Bake 45 minutes."

"Veal with Oysters

"Cut one pound of select veal into squares about the size of the oysters. Fry nice and brown and when done, add enough butter to make sufficient gravy and season. Pour over this one quart of oysters, well cleaned and drained, with two tablespoonfuls of flour stirred all through the oysters, and add pepper and salt. Cover and let steam until the oysters begin to curl and the gravy is thickened."

"White Soup

"Boil two quarts of meat broth; beat three eggs well; two cups milk; and two spoonfuls flour. Pour these gradually through a sieve into the boiling soup; salt and pepper to taste."

"Eggs A La Suisse

"Spread two ounces of fresh butter over the bottom of a dish, cover with grated cheese and break eight whole eggs upon the cheese without breaking the yolks. Season with red pepper and salt if needed. Pour a little cream over the eggs; sprinkle about two ounces of grated cheese over the top and place in a moderate oven for about fifteen minutes. Brown by passing a hot salamander over the top."

"Sweet Pickled Peaches

"Wash clean several pounds of peaches that are not too ripe; it is best to use clings and do not peel them. Put into a porcelain kettle three pounds of brown sugar, one pint of strong cider vinegar, and a small handful each of cinnamon and cloves and bring to a boil. Put in as many peaches as the liquor will cover; cook until moderately soft and put into jars. Cook all alike and pour liquor over them."

Chapter X

HELPS FOR THE KITCHEN QUEEN

There are books and more books of hints and shortcuts to make the work-a-day life of the mother and housewife a little lighter. From those books we have gleaned a few items which should lighten the heavy load of the homemaker. Each word of wisdom (circa 1850-1900) has been selected with care and consideration for the joy it can bring in lightened housework. In the day of Grandma, it meant more time for more work. Today it can mean more time for soap operas, bridge parties, and could even mean a little more time to read Horatio Alger, Tom Swift, The Rover Boys . . . and for a classic . . . *Little Women.*

"Washing Fluid
"One ounce of salts of tartar, one ounce of carbonate ammonia, one box Babbit's lye, one gallon of soft water. Use one-half teacup to a washing."

"To Clean Carpets
"One cake ivory soap, one bottle ammonia, five cents worth of ether. Dissolve soap in one gallon of hot water and when cool, add ammonia and ether. Scrub small space at a time with a brush and wipe dry with a soft cloth wrung out of warm water."

"Wall Paper Cleaner
"One-half cup water, one cup flour, three teaspoonfuls vinegar, three teaspoonfuls ammonia, one teaspoonful carbon oil. Boil and stir constantly until thick; work in small balls, and rub paper with downward strokes. Will not streak or spot if made as directed."

"To Destroy Odor of Burning Lamp Wicks

"Boil new lamp wicks in vinegar and then thoroughly dry them. There will then be no odor from them when burning."

"To Preserve Eggs

"One quart of salt, one pint of slacked lime, and three gallons of water. This liquid will keep eggs for years."

"To Remove Paint Stains

"Old dry paint stains may be removed from cotton and woolen goods by first covering the spots with olive oil or butter and then applying chloroform."

"To Purify Cistern Water

"Cistern water may be purified by hanging a bag of charcoal in the water."

"A Tight Shoe

"Wring a cloth out of hot water and apply to the part that is tight. If necessary renew and keep shoe on until the leather is stretched."

"To Remove Scorches

"Spread over the scorched places a mixture of the juice of two onions, two ounces Fuller's earth, and one-half pint of vinegar. These ingredients should be mixed, thoroughly boiled and cooked before using."

"To Keep Butter for Winter Use

"Into six pounds of fresh butter work a large spoonful of salt and a tablespoonful each of saltpeter and powdered white sugar. Pack in a crock that is perfectly clean and cover with salt."

"Fire-Kindler

"Soak corn-cobs in kerosene oil. When needed, put a cob in the stove, set fire to it and put on the fuel."

"To Destroy Worms and Slugs

"Spray the bushes with a solution of one pound of powdered hellebore to twenty-five gallons of water."

"Icy Windows

"Rub the glass with a sponge dipped in alcohol and the windows will be kept free from ice. Alcohol is also good to polish them."

"To Drive Away Ants

"Put a small bag of sulphur in the drawers and cupboards. Ants don't like sulphur."

"To Remove Smell of Paint

"Mix Chloride of lime in water, sprinkle hay with it and spread it in the room."

"To Clean A Sponge

"Rub fresh lemon juice thoroughly into a soured sponge, then rinse several times in warm water and the sponge will be as sweet as when new."

"To Keep Celery

"Bury it in dry sand."

"To Keep Onions

"The best way is to spread them over the floor."

"To Remove Tar

"Scrape off all the tar possible and then thoroughly wet the place with melted lard or salad oil and let it remain for twenty-four hours. If woolen or silk, take out the grease with either spirits of wine or ether. If cotton or linen, wash out in strong, warm soap suds."

"Gnats

"Camphor is the best preventive and cure for the stings of gnats."

"To Polish Patent Leather

"Orange juice will be found to be a good polish for patent leather."

"To Frost Window Panes

"Dissolve some epsom salts in beer and apply with a brush and you will have the best window frosting known."

"To Rid Moths

"Moths will not lay their eggs where fine-cut tobacco has been scattered."

"To Keep Mice Away

"Mice do not like the smell of camphor gum and if it is placed in drawers or trunks they will keep at a distance. Seeds may also be protected by mixing small pieces of camphor gum with them."

"To Get Rid of Flies

"You will not be troubled with many flies if you keep geraniums growing in the house. Then why not have more flowers and fewer flies?"

"To Make Hard Water Soft

"Fill the boiler with hard water and set on the stove. Put half a cup of wood ashes into a woolen bag covered with cotton cloth to prevent the sifting out of the ashes and hang the bag in the water until the water is warm."

"Hard Soap

"Put seven pounds of tallow, three pounds of rosin and two pounds of potash into six gallons of water and boil three to five hours. Pour into a wash tub and let it stand overnight. In the morning cut it into bars and lay in the sun for two or three days to harden. This will last an ordinary family a year and save many a penny."

"Soft Soap

"To six gallons of soft water add three pounds of best hard soap (finely cut), one pound of salsoda, and four tablespoonfuls of hartshorn. Boil until it is entirely dissolved. Pour into convenient vessels and when cold it will be ready for use. This makes fifty pounds of fine soft soap."

"To Clean Oil Cloth

"Instead of using soap and water, wash with sweet milk. The milk makes it look fresh and bright without destroying the luster."

"To Kill Bed Bugs, Moths, Etc.

"Hot alum water is the best thing known to destroy insects. Boil alum and water until it is dissolved then apply the hot solution, with a brush, to closets, bedsteads, cracks, or wherever insects are found. All creeping insects may be destroyed by its use. There is no danger of poisoning and its persistent use will rid you of the pests."

"To Remove Onion Smell from Breath

"Parsley, eaten with vinegar, will destroy the unpleasant breath caused by eating onions."

"To Mend Iron Vessels

"Mix finely some sifted lime with the white of an egg 'till a thin paste is formed, then add some iron filings. Apply this to the fracture and the vessel will be found nearly as sound as ever."

"To Clean Lamp Chimneys

"Hold chimney over the steam coming from a boiling kettle, then wipe it inside and outside with a soft muslin cloth."

"To Remove Wrinkles

"Melt and stir together one ounce of white wax, two ounces of strained honey, and two ounces of the juice of lily bulbs. Apply to the face every night and it is said your wrinkles will disappear."

"Remove Coffee Stains

"The yolk of an egg mixed with a little water will remove coffee stains. Glycerine will do the same. Rub out before washing."

"To Exterminate Roaches

"With a machine oil can, squirt kerosene oil into cracks and seams behind woodwork, then sprinkle powdered borax over the shelves and blow it into the cracks with a powder blower."

"To Remove Kerosene

"Cover the spot with cornmeal, lay a paper over it, and rub with a moderately heated iron. Two or three applications will remove the kerosene. Finely powdered chalk may be used instead of the cornmeal if desired."

Chapter XI

LAUGH, PIONEER, LAUGH

Since the days of Joe Miller and the days of the court jesters, there has been little change in jokes and humor. Even today, the pie-in-the-face routine and the ancient pratfall are standards on television and in moving pictures.

These jokes were gleaned from times as far back as the Civil War and reflect a never-changing trend. They are offered here just as they were printed when grandmother baked vinegar pie and grandfather smoked cigar clippings in his corncob pipe.

★　★　★

When Colonel Van Wyck was running for congress many years ago in the Fifteenth New York district, there was a certain Irishman who steadfastly refused to give the old soldier any encouragement. The colonel was greatly surprised, therefore, when Pat informed him on election day that he had decided to support him.

"Glad to hear it, glad to hear it," said the colonel. "I rather thought you were against me, Patrick."

"Well, sir," said Patrick, "I wuz, and whin ye stud by me pigpen and talked that day for two hours or worse, ye didn't budge me a hair's breadth, sir; but after ye wuz gone away I got to thinking how ye reached yer hand over the fence and scratched the pig on the back 'till he laid down wid the pleasure of it, and I made up me mind that whin a rale colonel was as sociable as that I wasn't the man to vote agin him."

[*Nebraska State Journal*]

★　★　★

"Ernest, what does 'amen' mean?" said Philip to his older brother, who had reached the wise age of six.

169

"It means mustn't touch it, Philip," was the unhesitating reply.

"Ernest!" exclaimed the boys' mother, who had overheard the question and answer, "why do you tell your little brother that?"

"You told me so, Mamma," answered Ernest.

"Why, no; think what you are saying. I could not have told you that," urged the astonished mother.

"But you did, Mamma. I asked you, and you said, 'Amen means mustn't touch it,' " returned the little boy, very positively. His mother was greatly puzzled until she remembered that she had said, "Amen means, so let it be."

★ ★ ★

Wife: "I hope you are pleased with those slippers, darling?"

Husband — (hesitatingly) — "Yes, dear, I'm so glad I learned to walk on snowshoes when I was a boy."

★ ★ ★

A young couple in a Lancashire village had been courting for several years. The young man said one day to the young woman, "Sal, I canna marry thee."

"How's that?" said she.

"I've changed my mind," said he.

"Well, I'll tell you what we'll do," said she. "If folks know that it's thee as has given me up, I shanna be able to get another chap, but if they think I have given thee up, then I can easy get another chap. So we'll have the bans published, and when the wedding day comes the parson will say to thee: 'Wilt thou have this woman to be thy wedded wife?' and thou must say, 'I will;' and then when he says to me, 'Wilt thou have this man to be thy wedded husband?' I shall say, 'I winna.' "

The day came and when the minister said, "Wilt thou have this woman to be thy wedded wife?" and the man answered "I will." Then the parson said to the woman, "Wilt thou have this man to be thy wedded husband?" and she said, "I will."

"Why," said the young man, furiously, "you said you would say, 'I winna.' "

"I know that," said the young woman, "but I've changed my mind since."

★ ★ ★

Herbert — "Really, Miss Edith, I am very sorry I kissed you. I didn't think what I was doing. It is a sort of temporary insanity in our family."

Miss Edith (pityingly) — "If you ever feel any more such attacks coming on, you had better come right here, where your infirmity is known, and we will take care of you."

★ ★ ★

"What a queer name you have, Miss Booglespeegle?" he said, after he had asked her once or twice to pronounce it for him.

"Well," she responded, with just the sweetest smile, "you know what you can do with that name, Mr. Smith."

★ ★ ★

Call a girl a spring chicken and she will laugh; call a woman a hen and she gets mad. Call a young lady a witch and she will enjoy it; call an old woman a witch and your life is in danger. Call a girl a kitten and she won't take it unkindly; call a woman a cat and she will hate you. Remarkable sex.

★ ★ ★

Hog and hominy is the popular dish in some portions of the south, just as pork and beans delight the palate of the New Englanders, and catfish and waffles appeal to the taste of Philadelphians.

How dearly a Virginian loves ham may be inferred by the following conversation, reported by a home-coming commercial traveler:

While riding from an interior town in the stage, he fell into conversation with the driver. The talk finally turned upon hunting, the driver informing his fare that the woods thereabouts

171

abounded in game. Passing a stream, the traveler asked if it contained fish.

"Lots of them," was the reply.

"What kind?"

"Mostly trout," said the driver. "All these mountain streams are full of trout."

"They must be fine eating," was the next remark.

"Fine eating," exclaimed the driver. "Well, I should say so. You just go up to the mountains and catch half a dozen trout, about ten or twelve inches long, clean 'em without washing 'em, rub in some salt, roll 'em in Injun meal and bake 'em in the ashes. Good eatin'! Why, stranger, they beat ham!"

★ ★ ★

Undoubtedly the cow that died recently in Comstock from eating too many apples had serious trouble in cider.

★ ★ ★

A Kentucky grand jury brought in an indictment in which it is stated that the defendant "did unlawfully, wilfully and maliciously kill and destroy one pig, the personal property of George Pigg, the said pig being of value to the aforesaid George Pigg. The pig thus killed weighed about 25 pounds and was a mate to some other pigs owned by said George Pigg, which left George Pigg a pig less than he (said George Pigg) had of pigs, and thus ruthlessly tore said pig from the society of George Pigg's other pigs against the peace and dignity of this commonwealth of Kentucky.

★ ★ ★

When Charles Dudley Warner was editor of the Hartford (Conn.) Press, in the "sixties," arousing the patriotism of the state by his vigorous appeals, one of the typesetters came in from the composing room, and planting himself before the editor, said: "Well, Mr. Warner, I've decided to enlist in the army."

With mingled sensations of pride and responsibility, Mr. Warner replied, encouragingly, that he was glad to see that the man felt the call of duty.

"Oh, it isn't that," said the truthful compositor; "but I'd rather be shot than try to set any more of your copy."

A little girl was visiting, in company with her mother, at the house of a neighbor. The tot gazed so constantly at the new bonnet of the hostess (an article that happened to be in full view) that the owner asked: "Do you like it, Laura?"

The innocent replied: "Why, mother said it was a perfect fright, but it doesn't scare me a bit."

★　★　★

One of the peculiarities of human nature is to ask a question that is exceedingly foolish. For instance, if one sees a friend knocked down by a coal cart, the first question that one is apt to ask is, "Did you get knocked down?" At Troost park last evening a gentleman was standing on the edge of the lake when he slipped and fell in. Naturally his temper was at a white heat. He glared about savagely, when a stranger, who was standing by and who had seen the accident, asked, "Did you fall in?"

The fellow paused, and, while his eyes were snapping fire, remarked sarcastically, "No, I didn't fall in. The lake sneaked up on me."

★　★　★

Mr. Younghusband — "My dear, I am sorry to see that one of your new dishes is cracked."

Mrs. Younghusband — "Yes, love, but what could you expect? We have had cracked wheat in it for the past three months."

★　★　★

After rapping two or three minutes to bring the chief clerk to his window yesterday, a well-known citizen blandly said, "I found this bunch of keys outside here; probably belong to some business man who was in after his mail."

"All right," said the clerk; and the bland-spoken man went out.

Fifteen minutes later he returned, rapped again, and just as blandly said, "Will you let me see those keys?"

"Yes, sir."

"Ah! they are mine! I discovered it after climbing three flights of stairs. Much obliged for helping me find them."

Gov. Green, of Trenton, N. J., tells a good story at his own expense. A few days ago while waiting for a train at the Elizabeth station, he engaged the services of a juvenile boot-black. As the youth plied his brushes the governor grew sociable and pleasantly inquired: "How's business, Johnnie?"

"Name ain't Johnnie," laconically answered the lad: "Name's Tommy."

Slightly taken back by Tommy's indisposition to be sociable, the governor said nothing for a while, but finally he remarked: "Well, Tommy I guess you don't know who I am, do you?"

"Yes, knowed you long ago," said Tommy.

"Well, who am I?"

"Yer Bob Green's father."

The President of the Association (interrupting the speaker to whisper in his ear) "Ex-Senator Windberg, your address is very interesting, but — er — you know the programme calls for only a few brief remarks."

Senator Windberg, (pulling out his watch) — "Certainly, I understand that, sir; and I shall keep within bounds. At present, you see, I have talked only three hours and a quarter."

Two young men, salesmen in a dry-goods store, hired bicycles and took a spin into the country. When they were perhaps ten miles out, they decided to have a race. One of them got far ahead of the other, and in dashing round a turn ran into a pile of stones. The wheel was demolished, and the rider found himself lying among the spokes. An aged woman who happened to be passing was met by the second rider.

"My good woman," said he, "have you seen a young man riding a bicycle on ahead?"

"No," said the woman; "but I saw a young man up the road a spell ago who was sittin' on the ground mendin' umbrellas."

A prominent charlatan of Chicago was conducting a class of his students through one of the hospitals of that city, when a patient was brought in, who, the attendants reported, was suffering from typhoid fever. "Ah! a terrible disease is typhoid fever," said the would-be professor. "Terrible! It either kills a patient or leaves him a complete idiot. I have had it."

★ ★ ★

The young man's father was paying him a visit, just to see how he was getting along at college. "So yer learin' fencin'?"

"Yes."

"That's right, William. Learn ter make yerself useful ter yer father. Don't bother none about rail fence. Stone fence is what they need in our section of the country."

★ ★ ★

A specimen son of the Emerald Isle was ushered into the dining-room at the dinner hour and the polite steward took hold of the back of the chair to push it into place. The guest looked around suspiciously for a minute, and then said loud enough to be heard all over the room: "By the howly Moses, if yez jerk that chair from under me I'll knock the whole top of yer head off."

★ ★ ★

A father was lecturing his son of the evils of late rising. "Remember," he concluded, "that the early bird catches the worm."

"And father," returned the boy, sarcastically, "how about the worm? Where was his reward for early rising?"

"I am informed," replied his father, gravely, "that the worm was on his way home, and hadn't been in bed at all."

★ ★ ★

An exchange says there are some things a level-headed human being shouldn't do. Among them is kindling a fire with kerosene, walking a railroad track, attempting to board a moving train, pointing a gun toward another, putting his name on another's notes, keeping his savings in an old stocking under the bed, playing a game of chance with a prepossessing stranger,

175

taking unknown medicines for real or imaginary ills, running for office when he has a paying position in private life, or calling a bigger man a liar.

★ ★ ★

The teacher of a kindergarten was mentioning some points of difference between cotton and wool, and goods made of those materials. Standing by a bright little four-year-old and gently stroking his coat sleeve, she said, "Now, Maynard, you never would dream that your little coat was made out of wool that came right off of a sheep's back, would you?"

He looked up into her face as if pitying her ignorance, and very promptly answered, "No, and 'twasn't either. 'Twas made out of papa's old pants.'

★ ★ ★

All sorts and sizes of people can find lodging nowadays at mountain and seaside resorts. A landlady advertises that she has "an airy, well-furnished bedroom for a gentleman twelve feet square." Another has "a desirable suite of rooms for a family in good repair." A third advertises "a bedroom for a single woman eight by twelve."

★ ★ ★

First boy — "Th' man at the railroad crossing is wavin' a red flag. What does that mean?"

Second boy (driving) — "That means we've got to hurry or we won't get across before the train comes."

★ ★ ★

Man is only an atom in the realization of the great cosmic plan, but he does not feel so at all when his new boots persist in squeaking as he walks down the church aisle a little late.

★ ★ ★

"And now, children," remarked Prof. Hailes in one of the board schools the other day, "If a family consisting of father and mother and seven children should have a pie for dinner, how much would each one receive?"

"An eighth part," answered a bright boy.

"But there are nine persons, you must remember."

"Oh, yes, I know that, but the mother wouldn't want any. There wouldn't be enough to go around."

★ ★ ★

"Are you a native of this parish?" asked a Scotch sheriff of a witness who was summoned to testify in court.

"Maistly, yer Honor," was the somewhat enigmatic reply.

"I mean were you born in this parish?"

"Na, yer Honor; I was na born in this parish, but I'm maist a native, for a' that."

"You came here when you were a child, I suppose you mean?" continued the sheriff.

"Na, sir; I'm jist here aboot sax year noo."

"Then how do you come to be nearly a native of the parish?"

"Weel, ye see, when I cam' here, sax year sin', I jist weighed eight stane, an' I'm fully seventeen stane noo: sae ye that aboot nine stane o' me belangs to this parish, an' the ether eight comes frae Camlachie."

★ ★ ★

Mrs. Gilpin called upon Squire McGill's wife the other evening, and in the course of conversation mentioned that she had just purchased a cuspidor.

"Dear me," said Mrs. McGill, "so you've bought one have you? I wanted to get one for Fanny, but she didn't seem to have any ear for music, so we finally gave it up."

Chapter XII

THE CHRISTIAN WORKERS CAME

This account of early missionary work was written for a Christmas edition of the *Morning Record*, Traverse City, Michigan, in 1899. The author's identity is not known but its recounting is a vital link in the chain of history. It will bring a better understanding of the hardships endured by church workers and educational leaders when the roads were trails and the lumberjack was king. The account is in reference to the Grand Traverse area of Michigan.

"Those who have made northern Michigan their home for the past thirty or more years, and have watched the growth of the area, have noted with pleasure the steady advance along intellectual and religious lines.

"Today, with its many church spires pointing heavenward and its schools calling hundreds of youths to their daily studies, cannot but afford satisfaction to those who take an interest in all that goes to make up the best side of social and educational life.

"Those who in their church homes are today enjoying the results of the faithful efforts of the early settlers can hardly realize what difficulties had to be overcome in years gone by, and what privations were suffered by those who first devoted themselves to the betterment of the city. Indeed many of the stories of life in the early fifties read more like romance than reality and it is hard to realize that the stories of brave deeds accomplished and dangers overcome are anything more than fairy tales.

"Especially strange and unreal seem the stories of the first religious ceremonies in the little settlements nestled in the

179

shadow of the dense pine forests that circled the shores of blue
Grand Traverse bay and stretched miles on miles away to the
south and east.

"Although the spiritual needs of the Indians had long been
recognized and cared for, the little band of white men and
their families at the head of Grand Traverse bay only knew
Sunday as the one day in the week when the mill was silent and
there was a chance to rest and visit, and enjoy themselves as
best they might. There was little enough to break the monotony
of their lives. When death came suddenly to a young man at the
camp on the Boardman river, there was no one to say a word of
prayer, but a rude coffin was hastily constructed from the rough-
hewn planks piled near the mill and a grave was dug on the
sandy plain not far from the bay shore. The body was laid away
without further ceremony.

"In the winter of 1852-53, a young man died at the boarding
house, and was laid to rest by the side of the lumberjack, funeral
services being conducted by Rev. H. C. Scofield, a young Baptist
minister who was spending a short time at East Bay. This was
the first religious service recorded as ever being held in Traverse
City. A burial service was read by A. T. Lay on the occasion of
the death of a Mrs. Churchill, soon after. Their resting place has
long since been invaded by the growing city, and the very spot
forgotten.

"The first preaching service in the place was conducted by
Rev. H. C. Scofield, and was a great novelty and source of entertainment to the children of the community to whom such
a thing was hithreto unknown. Their comments on the proceedings were decidedly disconcerting to the youthful divine,
who, however, kept on bravely to the end.

"From 1853 to 1857 there was no religious service held in
the Grand Traverse region with the exception of a Sunday
School conducted for a time by Mr. Scofield and Mrs. Dr. Goodale. As there were only eight scholars the lack of teachers was
not a source of difficulty and the chief trouble was to get the

youngsters to give up their good times among the huckleberry bushes long enough to study the lesson in the little old log building, formerly a barn, on Front street between Boardman avenue and Wellington street, which answered the double purpose of day school and church.

"In 1857 Rev. D. R. Latham of the M. E. church stopped at Old Mission on his way to Kansas and concluded that a field was waiting for him there which would repay his labors. A class was soon formed and a church organization followed. His audiences were of a somewhat unusual nature. The United States revenue cutter Michigan sometimes anchored in the harbor over Sunday and the blue uniformed officers mingled in the rude little church with poorly clad settlers and scarcely-clad-at-all Indians. One old chief, who was credited with having a chest full of white men's scalps in his wigwam, used to come in warm weather attired only in a shirt and breech-cloth, but preserving throughout the service the dignity of the traditional deacon, and another frequent listener to the gospel of love had been known in his early days to eat a human heart torn from the body of a victim of the Mackinac massacre.

"In the course of the summer of 1857, Rev. W. H. Brockway, on some sort of an expedition, found his way from the southern part of the state up through the woods to Old Mission, and falling in with Mr. Latham persuaded him to join the Michigan conference. As there was no quarterly conference at Old Mission to give the necessary recommendation, Mr. Brockway took his church letter to some Indian mission farther south, probably the one in Isabella county, where he was formally recommended to the annual conference.

"At the annual conference in 1857, two circuits were formed on Grand Traverse bay, Old Mission and Elk Rapids, and Northport and Traverse City. Mr. Latham was to supply the former and Rev. L. J. Griffin was appointed to the latter. On learning the relative situation of Northport and Traverse City, forty miles apart, Mr. Griffin wrote Mr. Latham, asking him to take Traverse City off his hands, which he consented to do. Mr. Griffin labored at Northport and Carp River, forming classes at those place, and Mr. Latham at Old Mission, Traverse City, and Elk Rapids.

"The first quarterly meeting of the circuit of which Mr. Latham was now the regularly appointed pastor, was held at Old Mission, the presiding elder, Rev. H. Penfield, being present. J. M. Pratt had been appointed class leader, and was the only official member on the circuit; the quarterly conference therefore consisted of only three, the presiding elder, the pastor, and the class leader. It is said that in making out the official list Mr. Latham made the nominations, Mr. Pratt did the voting, and the presiding elder declared the result.

"Mr. Latham organized a Methodist class in 1858 in the little new school building erected where Park Place Motor Inn now stands. There were seven members, and regular services were held by the faithful pastor, who taught at Old Mission during the week, preached there every Sunday morning, and then walked to Traverse City and preached in the evening, walking back afterward in time to open school Monday morning. One raw Sunday night in the middle of March, after preaching as usual, and then stopping at Mr. Hannah's for refreshments, he commenced his tiresome journey back to the Mission, taking a short cut across the ice to Bower's harbor. About two miles from the town he entered a heavy fog, and soon became bewildered. The Indians were indulging in a dance near the mouth of the river, and taking the sound of their drums for a guide he walked as nearly as possible in an opposite direction 'till he reached and passed the island, narrowly avoiding many dangerous openings in the soft ice. Here he followed the sound of an owl's hooting on the main land 'till he suddenly walked into the water covering the ice near the shore. Some Indians heard his cry for help, and he was finally rescued from his dangerous position.

"Another courageous pioneer minister was Rev. J. W. Miller who lived in a cozy residence on State street, and had a charge at Elk Rapids. Mr. Miller took charge of the Whitewater circuit in 1860, and though the funds of the young minister were heavily drawn upon by the expense of moving into the region, his parishioners evidently thought he and his wife would be cared for as was Elijah in the olden times, and neglected to supply the actual needs of the family 'till they often found themselves reduced to dining on potatoes and salt. With an undaunted courage Mr. Miller perservered in his good work, and the trials of pioneer life seem today more like a dream than a reality.

"No braver and more faithful man ever ministered to the wants of the whites and Indians alike in the early days of the region than Fr. Ignatius Mrak, who was loved and revered by Catholics and protestants alike. He came to northern Michigan in 1845 and in 1855 settled with his Indian charges at Peshabetown, then Eagletown, coming to Traverse City occasionally to say mass at the home of some of his parishioners here. During many a fierce storm of winter he trudged through the unbroken forest drifts on his snow shoes, dragging after him the little sledge containing the outfit for services and his provisions for the journey, wrapping himself up in his blanket as night came on and sleeping with the heavens for his only covering.

"The first two churches built in Traverse City were the First Methodist Episcopal and the Congregational. These were completed in 1867, the dedication of the Methodist church taking place in October and the Congregational following a few months later.

"In 1870 a Catholic church building was erected, which became too small for the rapidly growing parish, and in 1889 a new church was finished and dedicated.

"Between the building of the first churches and the present time many denominations have organized branches in the city and built for themselves pleasant church homes. At present [1899] there are twelve church buildings, the First and Second M. E., Congregational, St. Francis Catholic church, Baptist, Episcopal, German Lutheran, German Evangelical, Swedish Lutheran, Presbyterian, Friends, and the Seventh Day Adventist.

The Church of Christ (Disciples) meets in Grange hall, and the Church of Christ (Scientist) in their rooms on Union street. The Free Methodists hold meetings in the Fernwood chapel. The Hebrew congregation meets in its synagogue on Park street.

"Early school incidents are interesting. In November 1851, five young men arrived at Old Mission, in the schooner Madeline, with the intention of wintering in the vicinity. Three of them were brothers named Fitzgerald. A fourth was called William Bryce. The name of the fifth, who was employed by the others as cook, has been forgotten. The five were all good sailors and three of them had been masters of vessels during the past season but all were deficient in education. None of them were even tolerable readers, and one of the number was unable to write his name. An eager desire to learn was the occasion of their coming.

"At Old Mission, the man who had been engaged as teacher failing to meet the contract, S. E. Wait, then only nineteen years of age, was employed, at $20 per month and board. Bryce and the Fitzgeralds were to pay the bill, the cook receiving his tuition in compensation for his services. The Madeline was brought to Bowers' Harbor, and securely anchored for the winter. The afterhold was converted into a kitchen and dining-room. Regular hours of study were observed, and the men voluntarily submitted to strict school discipline. Out of school hours, they had plenty of exercise in cutting wood and bringing it on board, to say nothing of the recreation of snowballing, in which they sometimes engaged with the delight of genuine schoolboys. The bay that year did not freeze over until March. Previous to the freezing, the wood was brought on board in the yawl; afterwards it was conveyed over the ice. Except by way of Old Mission, to which occasional visits were made, the party was entirely cut off from communication with the outside world.

"The schools have kept pace with the religious growth of the city, and from the little beginning, with twelve scholars, in the log building on Front street, in 1853, has sprung the large present fine school system, with the central building, three com-

184

modious brick ward buildings and two smaller suburban buildings. The present (1899) enrollment in the schools is over 1900 and the last school census showed 2,464 children of school age in the city.

"The fame of the Traverse City schools has gone abroad, and a large number of non-resident pupils profit every year by the excellent course of study.

"Pupils passing a satisfactory examination in the prescribed courses are admitted to the University at Ann Arbor on their certificates."

Chapter XIII

"A-PIONEERING WE WENT"

by Mrs. J. G. Ramsdell

Mrs. J. G. Ramsdell was the wife of a pioneer fruit farmer in the Grand Traverse Region of Michigan. Mr. Ramsdell was circuit judge for the district in which he lived and Mrs. Ramsdell was very active in community improvement affairs. She frequently prepared papers which she presented to the members of The Old Settlers Association. This reminiscent piece was written in December of 1899, and gives a woman's understanding and acceptance of hardship and difficulty.

"In September of 1860, having decided to make a home for ourselves in the Grand Traverse region, we prepared to leave our home in Lansing where my husband, Mr. Ramsdell was practicing law.

"We shipped our household goods and library, by way of Jackson and Chicago, to Northport and took the Ramshorn railroad which had just then opened from Lansing to Owosso. Thence we went by D. G. H. & M. to Grand Haven. Our intention was to go from Grand Haven by steamer to Milwaukee, from there to Manistee by sail, and then across by trail to Traverse City.

"On reaching Grand Haven our plans were changed. The propeller Mears was in the harbor on its way down shore with a quantity of Lumberman's supplies (chiefly baled hay) to be delivered at Lincoln, 25 miles south of Manistee, and if the weather would permit, was to go around Big Point Sauble to Freesoil, only ten miles south of Manistee.

"We went on board the Mears and took our chances. It was a beautiful morning when we steamed out of the harbor on the lake. And my delight in the beautiful water trip was great. But the wind arose. The lake got rougher and rougher and the badly ballasted boat began to roll until, for eight long hours, I moaned and groaned too sick to raise my head until we rounded Little Sauble Point and entered Pentwater harbor, 50 miles from Manistee.

"Here the captain of the Mears informed us that he could go no farther down the shore and we would have to either go ashore there or go with him to Chicago, as he should leave his supplies there, load with lumber and go direct to that city.

"At that time the government carried a weekly mail between Muskegon and Manistee. It was a 'star route,' run by pony express, and we chanced to land at Pentwater in time to catch the stage en route to Manistee, so here was our chance, or rather my chance, as it afterwards proved. The mail boy was found. His horses were being shod and he could take the lady and the satchels but the gentleman would have to walk! In the course of half an hour the 'stage' came around to pick me up. It was drawn by a span of Indian ponies, in size about half way between a Newfoundland dog and a western broncho.

"Under the direction of the 'mail boy' (who wore a mustache and side whiskers) I mounted the cart and the seat which had all the spring of the axle and no more.

"So we started out of Pentwater for Manistee, the 'gentleman' walking behind. We expected to reach Lincoln that night but the fates were against us.

"It was dark when we passed the cliffs south of Pere Marquette lake and dark when we reached the beach beyond, but light enough so that I could see that we had both wheels in the water when the waves rolled in. I was on the lakeward side, but ready to spring the moment I felt the cart drop. Soon the shoreward wheels ran over some article, tilting the cart toward the lake, and I screamed and sprang, passed in front of the driver over the box and sailed through the air for shore carrying the

188

lines with me. No inducement could get me into that cart again that night.

"I walked with the 'gentleman' on the beach a mile and a half to the ferry. We arrived there after nine o'clock. The ferry was locked up on the farther shore. The wind was blowing a gale and the big lake was roaring fearfully. Call for the ferry was useless, but it brought some fishermen from their shanty near by. Their boats were all on the big lake side of the beach and to attempt to go through the breakers and around the pier was too dangerous even for them to undertake.

"There was a government life boat close by on the little lake but none other than government officers were allowed to use it. The key was left with them but they were instructed not to use it except in distress or to ferry government officers. 'Well,' said the gentleman, 'we have a double case then. We are in distress and I am a government officer, here is a dollar, get your key and take us across.'

"Whether it was the official air assumed or the dollar paid that commanded obedience is still in doubt but the life boat was soon ready. Then a new and unexpected difficulty arose. I balked! I absolutely refused to get into the boat. A sudden terror had seized me and the floating corpses of all the dead that had perished in that crossing swam out before me. To attempt that dangerous passage in the dark on such a night was suicide. Finally I compromised the matter by saying to Mr. Ramsdell, 'I will go if you command me to. I won't without, for I know we shall all be drowned.'

" 'Well,' said he, 'if that is all, it's easy enough. Get on that boat. There is no danger here under the bar.' So I got in, the fishermen took the oars and before I had time to faint or say my prayers we were safely landed on the north shore of the Pere Marquette river.

"There was no town then at Pere Marquette, (now Ludington). The mill was not running and the boarding house was occupied by a German and his wife, neither of whom could

189

speak a word of English, and our combined German consisted of yaw, nein, and nixfusta.

"We went to the boarding house and after about fifteen minutes of yawing, neining and nixfustaing, mixed with pantomime, we understood that we could get neither supper nor breakfast, but we could have a room and bed. After inspecting the bed, we considered it safer not to get inside of it, so without undressing we made a lounge of the bed and using shawl and overcoat for covering we put in the rest of the night.

"The next morning my driver was around with his stage in good season and we jolted off to Lincoln, four miles, to breakfast. Thomas Wood, who was in charge of the lumbering business at Lincoln, received us cordially, treated us right royally and, after breakfast, sent us on our way rejoicing.

"It was a case of welcoming the coming and speeding the departing guest that we could appreciate for he loaned my husband a horse to carry him to Manistee which the driver was to return on his southward trip.

"I mounted the cart and we slowly wended our way over hills and logs, and forded rivers and brooks for there were no bridges on the road.

"We reached Manistee that afternoon and spent a week visiting friends and making acquaintances and then prepared to resume our journey which was to be on horse back.

"All extra luggage was sent by boat to Chicago and then on to Traverse City. D. C. Filer loaned me his riding horse 'Turk' and Mr. Ramsdell borrowed his brother's horse 'General.' The General was a rather fine looking bay horse but a hard trotter and an awkward, wallowing galloper. The Turk was a sorrel of fine form, graceful motion, easy rider and the very perfection of equine intelligence.

"We started about 2:00 o'clock in the afternoon, headed for Portage ten miles this side of Manistee where we were to spend the night. At Portage we met Frank Hannah, brother of Perry Hannah of Traverse City, on his way out. From that place we took the beach to Herring creek.

190

"The only difficulty we found on the beach was the land-slides These were places where large patches of earth and trees had slid down the bluffs into the lake, blocking the beach and compelling a circuit around them into the water. These varied in width from a few feet to many rods. The water was shallow and, with quiet water there was no trouble in riding around them. But in a storm the passage was dangerous as the waves might throw horse and rider upon the roots and broken limbs of the trees.

"Shortly after we started the wind began to rise and the waves rolled higher and higher on the beach, so we made haste to reach and pass the bluffs between the bar and Herring Lake as this was the place where the landslides were the worst. When we came to the slides I obeyed Mr. Riler's injunction, dropped the reins, clung to the saddle, and "Turk" did the rest. We would strike in behind a receding wave, dash around and out before the next wave came in, if the distance was short, but where it was too great for that, he would hustle until the wave was nearly upon us, then turn facing it and rear so as to lift me entirely above the crest and as soon as it passed he would come down and scamper until the next one came, then repeat the operation until the landslide was passed."

Chapter XIV

BEFORE THE RAILS AND TELEGRAPH

This piece was written by Thomas Bates and recounts his recollections when the wildnerness was really wild. Mr. Bates was editor of the first newspaper in northern Michigan, The *Grand Traverse Herald,* and was a vitrolic and determined Republican. Herein he recounts his impressions of Traverse City in 1862. The text is exactly as he wrote it, unabridged.

"July 7, 1862 was a perfect 'Traverse' day. The air was tempered by a faint north wind and laden with the spicy odor of pines. For at that time the timber was still standing close to the bay-pines on the lower levels and various hardwoods on the higher reaches of shore.

"As the propeller Alleghany, with her peculiar 'list' to port, came snorting up the bay, just as the sun emerged from the forests of the peninsula, she seemed to have that wise manner of a monster who knew a thing or two. She dipped sideways in the water like an old salt who rolled a bit.

"It was at precisely this moment that I received my first impression of Traverse. I came out on deck, where Captain Baldwin stood talking to my father. The captain turned his shrewd eyes quizzing on me and said: 'Well, my boy, what do you think of your new home?'

" 'Where is it?' I asked, looking about. To the right rose a bank of woods; to the left, a range of forest; to the rear the island stood defined. And in front of us there was a notch in the monotony of timbered landscape — as if a snag-toothed giant had humorously bitten a piece out of the shoreline and disliked the flavor of it. Far away, puffs of whitish vapor were borne along, in low hanging clouds.

" 'There it is,' said my father, watching me closely. 'That is Traverse City.'

" 'I don't see any city,' said I. And that unpleasant fact was forced out of me, against my inclination and desire; for this was a mighty event — this 'coming to Traverse,' for it was my start into the great world.

"For several years we had talked of 'going west,' and Traverse City was naturally the objective point, because my father's twin brother, Morgan Bates, had located there in 1858 and started the *Grand Traverse Herald*. I was to enter his office as an apprentice.

"I was a native of Albany, New York — that oldest of cities in the country, save St. Augustine. To my youthful mind, a city meant a considerable community, and 'Traverse City' had been imagined to be a place of no mean importance. Therefore, it was not strange that a good deal of self control was needed to conceal my disappointment and not dampen the ardor of my father, whose happiness would be affected by my actions. I remember vividly how I felt on turning aside from the little group of busy men on the deck of the Alleghany. But youthful hopes were more vital than dispelled illusions. There was a tonic in the glorious air and the magnificent bay that toned the mind to meet th inevitable.

"We landed at the dock and crawled along through the piles of lumber to the sawdusted highway. The Traverse City I then saw was composed of some dozen or so buildings.

"First the saw mill, and next stood a partly dismantled grist mill. Then came three wooden structures, as we walked westward, which were the stores of Hannah, Lay & Co. These were built side to side, making a building 90x90 feet in size, the center one being of two stories. The boarding house and a barn-like house were west of the two stores, and a small frame shop over the way. Turning southward, we crossed a wooden bridge, and out diagonally through the sand to what is now the corner of Front and Cass streets. There were no buildings on the north side of Front street. At the corner of Union and Front streets stood the old Cutler residence, with a small house just west of it. Immense piles of slabs filled all the space from Union street up to Dr. Goodale's house, which stood where is now the Hotel Whiting. The Spraque residence was where Prokop Kyselka's store now stands. Across Cass was the Herald office. Then came the Smith Barnes house, the Goodrich house, the Fowle house, (afterward the 'Exchange') and then open lots until the little buildings on Park and Front were reached. These were occupied by Theron Bostwick, county clerk and register. An old log house stood near the corner of Front and Wellington, and James K. Gunton's noticeable hotel marked the eastern limits of the town.

"A small school house stood where is now the annex of Park Place and in the far off suburbs to the southeast, Morgan Bates had ventured to defy the wilderness and erect his home, still standing, and now the residence of Judge Lorin Roberts. He called the place 'Saint's Rest,' — but I never knew precisely why.

"A jail stood on the site of the present fine county buildings. It was of square hewn logs, and seldom occupied.

"To the west of what was then the town, Mr. Hannah lived; and beyond him lay a bunch of slab shanties, known as 'Bagdad.' There were the Company's barns and hay sheds in that region. The original mill still stood at the north of the pond, where now are built the populous south and west sides; but on the wide plain to the south, not a house existed.

"Judge Ramsdell's home was perched on his beautiful hill, and to the extreme east, the Bryant place was seen in the 'bight of the bay.' Only this, and nothing more. A small bridge crossed the Boardman at what is now the head of Boardman avenue. This dropped to pieces the next year and then the only way to get over to the plains south of the river was to cross on the rolling logs that usually filled the river, or go around by 'Bagdad' and so across the creek at the old mill. In 1862 there were but few

195

forms of diversion or recreation available in Traverse City. Everyone was too busy with the sterner duties of life to engage in pleasuring. Occasionally, during the winter season, a sleigh ride was indulged in, and a dance at the stopping place, but there was very little of that sort of social intercourse. Nearly all of the men were employed by Hannah, Lay & Co., in mill or store, and the women were too worn out with the day's struggle to keep these men fed and supplied with actual necessaries of life to care much for pleasure. Where everyone saw everyone during the day, there was no special inducement to play at meeting each other 'socially.' However, there was an occasional bit of jollity here in those early times. Perhaps some of the older residents will recall the incident of the 'big mitten.' There was a dance proposed, but for some reason the ladies refused to go. The gallants secured one of the Company's big lumber trucks; stuffed a huge mitten with sawdust; paraded this token of disapproval up and down the one street, and then buried the mitten, I think on the river bank, to the dirge of circular saws and Indian plaints.

"The village plat was an area of sandy waste, covered with blackened pine stubs, stumps and huckleberry bushes. Coarse brakes grew rankly wherever there was an odd corner, and trailing arbutus appeared under log and covert in profusion.

"The most noticeable bird was the beautiful bluejay. At night the whip-poor-will intensified the sense of loneliness by its incessant cry. I remember lying awake and listening to the mournful iteration of that creature's demand, with its interrupted note as if forced to swallow, until I was nearly frantic. The woods jutted so closely on my uncle's house, where I then lived, that the hot summer nights seemed to arouse a thousand wierd sounds — the dropping of the acorns on the roof — the whirr of insects and the chirping of small unseen beings of mysterious nature.

"I think, however, the most lonely suggestion that came to my boyish mind was the winter landscape on a moonlight night. The absolute stillness and the glitter of the spotless mantle that covered all the earth carried a vague message of our remoteness and the vaguer feeling of infinity. There was never seen a whiter moonlight, nor a bluer arch of heaven than at such a time.

"In the spring, when the lumber camp broke up and the men who had been for six months imprisoned in the pine woods, came down with 'the drive,' there was a renewal of life in the tiny settlement. As the last stretch was made and the first logs set adrift in Boardman lake, the 'gang,' with canthooks and pikes on shoulder, would come marching in, to the rhythm of a French song. The managers of the business liked to have the men come home in such a merry mood.

"If one wished to 'go somewhere,' there were no liveries to supply the order by 'phone. Horses were as rare as the idea of a wire message then. William Fowle owned a team of terrible steeds that made one fancy oneself on the traditional rail, and I have a vivid recollection of trying to keep on the upper deck of one of them. That year Morgan Bates bought a horse which rivaled Don Quixote's, much to my disgust, as I never admired imitations of the old knight. Mrs. Perry Hannah owned 'Roan Billy,' a neat little chunk of a beast when he wanted to be nice, and drove him to an open buggy. With these exceptions, as I remember the situation, our riding was done afoot or by ox team.

"We got one mail a week, over the mysterious trail, from a point somewhere near 'outside,' as the world beyond the horizon of Traverse was termed.

"An Indian, on foot in summer or on dog sledge in winter, brought in a pouch of mail matter. Traverse City was only a way-station. Old Mission, or 'Grand Traverse,' was the end of the route. The post office was in 'Bagdad,' at the slab shanty of Charles H. Marsh. He was a lawyer, with a mother who could read the addresses at least. We — that is, perhaps half a dozen persons — were wont to congregate at Marsh's about sundown of a Saturday night and wait the passing of that Indian. If the hour of ten came before he did, Mother Marsh used to turn us out and declare the post office suspended pro tem. But if the carrier

197

got there first, all we had to do was to sit still and patiently listen to colloquy between Marsh and his mother, pending the sorting of the mail. As a messenger for the Herald and the United States Land Office, most of the contents of that pouch were finally dumped into my market basket. Then I trudged through two miles of sand, sawdust or snow, as the case might be, to the house of 'Saint's Rest.' Letters were the chiefest blessing of that period; although newspapers were not amiss, since we knew by report that a war was going on far to the south. Grand Traverse sent its quota, and more, to the Union cause.

"Among the first to go was a young man employed on the *Herald*, Lewis Patrick. He died the following winter.

"The simple annals of this quiet settlement do not read like a startling story, but they were important to the people of the village then. Possibly one of the incidents of that year is more vivid than any other, and that is the attempted assassination of James K. Gunton by a drunken man named French, the night of July 4. There had been a celebration in the woods — on the site of the present home of Joseph A. Moore, on Washington street, that day. About midnight Mr. Gunton awakened my uncle, who was a justice of the peace, and told him that French had fired through an east window of the Gunton house, intending murder. It was a very close call for the genial landlord. I remember seeing Mr. Gunton and my uncle disappear among the dense growth of trees and bushes that arose between the two homes. I expected to hear another shot, indicating the presence of the assassin. But no unhappy event transpired. French fled the country, and the matter served for many a day to keep alive the tongues of the people.

"From these casual comments on the past, possibly your readers may gain some clearer idea of the primitive times, before Traverse City fulfilled the promise of its title and became the metropolis of a favored region — a city of no mean fame."

Chapter XV

POSTAL SERVICE AT THE BEGINNING

Indians were mail carriers and letters were few and far between. H. D. Campbell was assistant to the first postmaster in Traverse City, Michigan, when the makeshift station was established. Here, in his own words, is the story of the mail and how it was delivered into a wilderness country. It could well have been your community!

"Perhaps no other branch of our government, or even private industry shows the advance of civilization more than do the advances made by the United States mail service.

"Since the earliest settlements in America, post offices have existed. In 1639 postal service was recognized in Massachusetts, and maintained by private enterprise. In Virginia, postal service was performed at the expense of the planters in 1657, and in 1672 mail service was established between the several colonies. At this time there was regular mail service once a month between Boston and New York.

"In 1737 Benjamin Franklin was postmaster in the city of Philadelphia, and continued in the post office more than forty years.

"One of the first acts of the continental congress was the establishment of post offices and post routes between Falmouth, Maine, and Savannah, Georgia, for carrying intelligence and letters throughout the continent, and to spread the knowledge of the acts of congress and the progress of the revolution among the different colonies. This congress established the general post office and appointed Benjamin Franklin the first postmaster general.

201

"The rates of postage fixed in 1792 were continued for quite fifty years, when the letter postage was from six cents to twenty-five cents on each letter, according to the distance letters were carried. These high rates amounted almost to a prohibition of correspondence; therefore from that time to about 1840 the increase in mail service scarcely kept pace with the growth of population.

"As a matter of fact, the post office and postal service for the use of the people, and as the agency of the government, in which there is a greater interest than in any other department, is the product of the present generation.

"The rapid growth of the postal service is due to the reduction in letter postage, the introduction and extension of railroads by which greater dispatch is secured over the old methods of transportation, the introduction of the free delivery system in cities; and the increased efficiency in the management throughout the whole system; and the greater activity and stimulus from the business of the country.

"So in our own state (Michigan) the advance of the pioneer has been closely followed by the United States mail service. For instance, an aged friend of mine in his boyhood days was a clerk in the Detroit post office, when the entire mail for Michigan and great territory west of Detroit was carried upon one Indian pony's back, leaving Detroit once a week. Today one can hardly comprehend the immensity of mail matter now handled by rail and otherwise throughout the vast domain west of Detroit. All this has come about in the lifetime allotted to man.

"This part of Michigan, north of the Muskegon river, was, prior to 1850, an unbroken wilderness, with but one post office, then known as the Grand Traverse post office, located at what is now Old Mission, without any post route to connect with any mail service. The nearest office on the south was Croton, on the Muskegon river, one hundred and twenty miles directly south, and Mackinaw on the north, at about one hundred miles' distance. An old and well-defined Indian trail between these points over which the Indians were sent from the upper peninsula once during the close of navigation for all mail matter that might accumulate at Croton for this north country, and all mail for this neighborhood (Traverse City) was carried past us to Grand Traverse post office, twenty miles away.

"To illustrate the convenience of mail facilities here in the early days a little experience of the writer will explain.

"I came here in the fall of 1852, about the time of the presidential election that fall, and about the first of March the following spring a squad of twenty Indians and as many dogs came from the upper peninsula on their way to Croton for the United States mail and in due time returned, the Indians upon snow shoes, with packs of mail and camping outfit, in Indian file, thus packing the snow into a well beaten path for the dog trains to follow. Usually three to six dogs are harnessed in tandem to a sledge similar in form to our toboggan sledges, with mail bags, supplies, etc., bound to them. One Indian follows in the rear to see that all is well as the train a mile or more in extent moves along forward.

"On this occasion the mail for Traverse City was carried also and distributed at the Grand Traverse post office, and it happened that Ann Dakin, a domestic at the Boarding House (now Pangborn Hotel), was visiting at the Old Mission. So she received the mail for this place, (over a hundred pounds), strapped it on her back and brought it to the head of the bay. In this mail we received the news that General Franklin Pierce had been elected president of the United States, and was on the fourth of March duly inaugurated into that high office in Washington.

"While we received mail but once during the close of navigation, we frequently had opportunities of sending letters out to kindred and kind friends by some person from the north on his way over the trail to the outside world, who would take our letters for fifty cents apiece and mail them. These chances were gratifying, though at times expensive. Upon one occasion

I gave a man a ten dollar gold piece to take a box containing a present to my mother and express it at Muskegon. You may query now how I could trust a stranger with so valuable a package. My answer is, we did not have dishonest neighbors in those days. All believed in honesty as the best policy.

"Traverse City post office was established in 1853 with post route from Muskegon up the lake shore via Whitehall, Ludington, Manistee to Sleeping Bear, thence through the woods to Traverse City and over the trail to Grand Traverse (now Old Mission) with semi-monthly mail service.

"The late Dr. D. C. Goodale was appointed postmaster with the writer assistant. The doctor in order to qualify, in company with his bondsmen, W. M. McKhillip, now of Muskegon, and the late Thomas Cutler, went to Old Mission, a two days journey over the trail. During their absence the first mail arrived, being packed through from Manistee by one Peter Greensky, a faithful Indian mail carrier, and the writer had the honor of distributing the first United States mail in the Traverse City post office. The mailbag contained seven letters and several newspapers for this office. The cost of transportation over this route was four hundred dollars a year. The revenue of the office the first year was three dollars, all of which was expended for an office stamp.

" 'To the victor belongs the spoils,' so in President Lincoln's administration Yours Truly was appointed successor to succeed Dr. D. C. Goodale in the post office. At this time the revenue of the office had increased to about one hundred and fifty dollars a year. A year later, in 1862, having become interested in the establishment of post routes, post offices, and mail service in the northern counties, I resigned my commission and gave special attention to the increased demand for more and better mail facilities.

"During these early years our mails were carried by trusty Indians. The only precaution taken was a charge not to get drunk while in the mail service. We used to subject them to kiss the Bible, (as often as otherwise would be a pocket diary),

204

that he would keep sober while making a trip. I have yet to learn of the first violation of this solemn obligation.

"For many years from 1851 some of our letters were brought to us during the season of navigation from Chicago by lumber vessels or steam craft making regular trips between Chicago and Traverse City, a source of convenience to many living in this vicinity.

"An incident in this connection in 1862, while I was yet postmaster, that has never been made a public matter, may not be out of place to mention now, shows how contemptible an evil-disposed person can be under certain circumstances.

"This person had reported to the post office department that boats making regular trips between Chicago and Traverse City were then, and had been, carrying United States mail unauthorized between these points, and papers and instructions were sent to me as postmaster to investigate and arrest the officers and owners of the boats handling mail without authority.

"As a matter of fact, everybody living here was more or less accommodated by this gratuitous act on the part of the boat's officers and owners in question.

"No person except it might have been myself could have any well founded grievance from this cause and that only in so far as it might affect my commission in the post office bussiness. So I concluded to assume the role of judge and jury and pocket the papers and keep mum unless forced to take action at some future time, and the papers have never been served to this day.

"The first daily mail service was put in operation by the writer between Big Rapids and Traverse City, via Sherman in 1870, requiring four days time for a round trip. In 1873 mails were brought by rail from Clam Lake, (Cadillac) by my agents, thus giving us daily mails from Detroit and Chicago in twenty to twenty-four hours in place of three days per contract schedule time.

"Since 1874 much of our mail service has been performed by railroad service bringing our mails several times daily. All of

205

this has helped to increase the business of the Traverse City post office which is second to none of the many offices located north of the Muskegon river today.

"See the comparison of the first year's business and the last year's business of the office, viz:

1853 — Revenue, $3.00; Expenditures, $3.00.

1898 — Revenue, $13,816.75; Expenditures, $6,104.76."

Chapter XVI

WILDERNESS WATER

Perry Hannah was the founder of the city of Traverse City, Michigan. He was a colorful "Kentucky Colonel" type of person who hacked a hole in the wilderness, built a mill, established a mercantile business, and became a part of the community, not only in the pioneer days, but down through the years. Busy as he was, he took time out to pen these reminiscences before the turn of the century.

"The young of today look to the early pioneer settler as one who had to endure great privation and experience untold hardships. This was not true with the first people of Grand Traverse. I never saw a happier or a more contented crowd than were the pioneers of Traverse. It seemed to me that they must all have taken lessons of John Stewart Mill, who said that he learned to seek his happiness by limiting his desires rather than attempting to satisfy them. I never spent more pleasant hours in my life than I did with the dozen or two that made up our entire number the first year.

"Last winter Mr. Vanderbilt was asked what he would choose for a Christmas present. His reply was, 'Give me an appetite.' It could not be furnished. Wealth could not buy it. No one ever complained in the early days in Traverse of suffering from such complaint. We were all happier than was the millionaire.

"In the first days of May, 1851, I left Chicago on the little schooner 'Venus,' in company with Captain Harry Boardman, a rich old farmer who lived in DuPage county, about five miles southeast of Naperville. The captain, two years before, had furnished his son with money to plant a mill on the little creek in the western part of our town, but experience had taught him that it would take more than the avails of one Illinois farm to sustain an operating mill with the present prices of lumber, hence he gave our firm an option for the sale of the mill and his landed estate, that is now Traverse City.

"Captain Peter Nelson, one of the finest old Dane sailors that ever walked on the deck of a ship, was master of the little schooner 'Venus,' and who will be known to many of our present settlers as manager of the lighthouse at Northport, of later years.

"We had left Chicago on our journey to the north but two or three days, when we met one of those terrible northeast gales, which were always sure to last full three days. We were well down Lake Michigan, and our brave old seaman decided that we must weather out the storm instead of returning, and never a more terrific time did I see in my life than those three days, pounding backward and forward across Lake Michigan. As soon as the gale subsided, we wended our way along into Grand Traverse bay, on one of the pleasantest, more beautiful and charming evenings that ever was seen; we rounded into the Old Mission harbor, just as the sun was going down behind the tops of the tall maples that stood on the ridge in the center of the Peninsula. It was one of those serene and beautiful evenings, with the southerly breeze not more than half a mile per hour — as we entered the harbor — and on the banks of the western side sat perhaps forty or fifty old Indian hunters. I could see with my glass that each one had his pipe in his mouth, and they were sitting on the bank watching the movement of our ship, chatting and talking as happy as one ever could imagine. To the rear of them were perhaps forty or fifty nice whitewashed wigwams, and around them could be seen the Indian women doing the drudgery of the night, and the Indian children hallooing here and there in their evening skips of play. Further up, in among the tall maples, could be seen the large white mansion of Rev. Peter Dougherty. Further up, beyond that, the Indian ponies, with their bells on their necks — their fore feet shackled together — were jumping from place to place, looking for the last meal for the night. Still further up were the great tall maples down behind which the sum was disappearing. I said to myself as I looked upon that beautiful scene that if 'ignorance is bliss, it is folly to be wise,' for a more beautiful picture I never saw in my life.

"After landing a few traps that we had brought for Mr. Dougherty, we wended our way around the turn; and as Captain Nelson was nearly worn out, he laid himself down on a blanket by the wheelman, ordering him to keep straight down the bay until he was well past the Mission point, and then call him.

"In a moment's time the old captain, tired out as he was, was well along in the 'land of nod,' and the good-hearted sailor seeing how nicely he was sleeping, thought it cruel to waken him and he could steer the ship around into West Bay without any difficulty. In a few moments, thump, thump, thump, went the little ship over the rocks. In a moment's time the old captain was on his feet, and then, I tell you, all was blue! We had run over a ledge of rocks into a pond, where there was plenty of water, and how to get out was the great sequel. After using the lead-line and sounding all around, the captain determined that the ship must be hauled back exactly in the same place that it went in, hence all hands had to work. The anchors were carried out in the small boats, and with the aid of a little extra south wind that had raised the water, we were able to get our boat back into its proper position, just as the sun was coming over the great green maples between Torch lake and the bay.

We wended our way around safely, up the West bay, viewing the beautiful shores as we skimmed along, seeing the green branches dipping over into the bay, which formed another of the beautiful pictures to be seen in those early days. About the middle of the afternoon we reached our moorings alongside of a little slab dock that was built in the western part of the bay.

"We soon made our way up to the mill. There we met the captain's son, but all hands were taking a little rest. As there had been a shower an hour before, and the boys couldn't work outdoors, the good-natured son had stopped the mill, allowing all hands to go in and have a game of euchre. This made the old captain — Harry Boardman — more willing than ever to sell, as he was fully satisfied that there was not quite push enough on Horace to make a successful lumberman.

"The next move was to prepare the packs for a trip up the Boardman (which we named after old Captain Harry) to ascertain if there was lumber sufficient on its banks to afford to locate a larger mill at the mouth of the Boardman. We journeyed up on the west and south side of the river to a point about where Mayfield now stands, crossing over to Hog's Back Lake, and thence down again — making up our minds that we had seen fifty millions of timber. Since that time, over four hundred millions have been cut and brought down the Boardman. Thus commences the beginning of the earliest days of Traverse City, and today we count ten thousand inhabitants.

"I have been often asked if I am not surprised at the great change which has taken place in these forty years. I can only answer that my expectations have not been realized. I looked forward within ten years to see a town here of twenty thousand inhabitants. I had seen cities grow up on the western prairies in less time, of greater size; but I did not take into consideration the great maples and elms which covered our country, and that it would take time to clear them away. It was considered in those days a great task to get rid of them, never expecting to see them worth what they are today. Yet I do believe that many of the people of today will see the time when Traverse City will reach its twenty thousand inhabitants; and I shall stay a little time longer, seating myself in an easy chair, in the afternoon of my life — watching Traverse City grow, believing that it will be one of the most beautiful towns in the state of Michigan."

Chapter XVII

AN OLD SETTLER SPEAKS

S. E. Wait was a settler in northern Michigan in 1850. He owned and operated the pioneer drug store in Traverse City, Michigan, for many years and was well known as a photographer. He was an excellent speaker and delivered this address to the seventeenth annual meeting of the Old Settlers Association on June 3, 1898.

"We meet here on the seventeenth anniversary of the Old Settlers Association to greet each other and shake hands. While the membership may not be growing less, yet each year finds us with fewer of the old settlers in attendance. And at each succeeding meeting, we miss some of the old familiar faces of the earlier days. We are all the time making history; but it is not history peculiar to our section. We are a part of the whole country and what is history with us today, is history of the whole, and it would be much more difficult to sift out of the past year what would be of local interest, than from a dozen of the earlier years.

"The early history of Grand Traverse county has been pretty thoroughly recorded and I have found it very difficult to find anything that has not already been told. So I will not try to get anything out of the past year but will go back and gather up some things that I think have not hitherto been noticed.

"Immigration seemed to take a special impulse towards this region in the fifties. The schooner *Arrow* owned at Old Mission by Cowles & Campbell, made weekly trips between Old Mission and Mackinaw bringing settlers each time, and in the fall of 1850 one trip was especially noticeable, she being so loaded with

213

household goods that her rigging was tied full of chairs, and the lighters articles that could not be stowed on deck or in the hold.

"Not being large enough to meet the demands of travel, her owners set about devising some plan to increase the capacity of the *Arrow* and lengthen her.

"Accordingly, late in the fall, they took her to the head of the west bay, up the Boardman river to the bend, and drew her out on the flat where the Asylum creek now flows into the river. They cut her in two, drew the two ends apart, and by the aid of whip saws and the little sawmill located on the creek, which supplied its power, lengthened her twelve feet during the winter of '50 and '51. In the spring she came out a trim schooner, sixty feet in length and having a capacity sufficient for the trade.

"In the latter part of April, 1853, the schooner *Active*, of Green Bay, anchored in the harbor at Old Mission with whiskey aboard and began to sell it to the Indians. As this was contrary to the principles of the whites there, it was decided to arrest the captain. Accordingly a constable, M. S. Wait, together with Dr. Babcock and John Fountain, took a boat and went on board for that purpose. When they were serving the papers, the boat was set adrift, the anchor weighed, sails set, and the schooner sailed away, sails set, to where nobody knew. A few days later, Lewis Miller arrived from Green Bay, and stated that they had been landed there. In due time, they arrived at home fully satisfied that it was a difficult matter to arrest a man on his own craft at anchor in public waters.

"On May 2nd, 1853, the steamer *Fashion* arrived at Old Mission from Detroit with the sheriff who had O. P. Hughson in charge who had been arrested for the murder of his nephew. The examination took place on the 3rd and he was bound over to the next term of the circuit court on July 26th. The judge, George Martin, not arriving on that date, the court adjourned unil his arrival, which occurred on the 28th at Traverse City, The prisoner made his escape on the same evening and nothing definite has ever been heard of him since.

214

"On the night of August 22nd, 1855, the peaceful village of Old Mission was considerably agitated by the arrival of a boatload of Mormons from Beaver Island, believed to be on an errand of plunder. During the night a shot was fired and a man was wounded. In the morning nothing was left to tell that they had been there other than a few drops of blood.

"In the fall of 1857, the government lands on the Peninsula were placed in the market and the land office, being located at Duncan in Cheboygan county, a few of the settlers decided to go and secure their claims. I copy the following from my journal written at that time:

" 'Old Mission, October 22nd, 1857. Charles Russell has just returned from the land office with the report that the fractional lands around Old Mission harbor have been placed in market, and J. M. Pratt, Dr. Fearnside, Porter Campbell, Jake Rickley, Capt. Shepard and myself intend starting for Little Traverse bay in the morning in Jack's boat, the Post-Boy.

" 'Little Traverse bay, October 23rd, 1857. It is now half past ten P.M. We have just landed at Harbor Point and are preparing to make a fire on the sandy beach. We left Old Mission at 6:00 this morning, stopped at New Mission at nine, took our noon lunch off Pine river, and by the aid of a gentle breeze and our oars, have just reached here.

" 'Indian village on Burt's lake, October 24th. We crossed Little Traverse bay early this morning, landed near an Indian village where we built a fire and cooked our breakfast. We heard that two Indians were going to the Indian village on Burt's lake and, after eating, with them as our guide, we started off at a brisk rate, climbing very steep hills and following an extremely crooked trail until about noon when we arrived at a small brook, quenched our thirst in its clear waters, and proceeded on our way. Reaching the shore of the lake at 4:00 o'clock, we dropped down from sheer fatigue and, after resting awhile, proceeded to the village about a quarter of a mile distant. We built a fire and ate our supper with a relish suitable to the occasion.

" 'We have bought two log canoes of the Indians and intend to make the rest of our trip by water. The sky is clear and the lake looks beautiful by moonlight.

" 'Cheybogan, October 25th. The wind being fair, we rigged our blankets for sails and left the village at nine. We crossed the lake about four miles to the head of Indian river which joins Burt's and Mullet lakes, took down our sails, and started down the swift current of the stream. About half way we met the mail carrier going to Grand Traverse. On arriving at Mullet lake, the wind blew so fresh in our faces, that we were discouraged about attempting to cross the lake. However, after eating a lunch, we made the attempt and succeeded. We followed the shore, cutting across from point to point, reached the head of Cheybogan river just about dusk, and had to descend the stream by starlight. On reaching the village we unloaded our blankets, etc., and walked about half a mile to the house where we are putting up for the night. The keen north wind that comes across the straits renders the evening air extremely chilly.

" 'Black river camp, October 26th. After breakfast this morning, we crossed the river in a boat and went to Duncan along the worst corduroy road I ever saw. On inquiry, we found that our lands were not in market, but only the lands belonging to the Presbyterian mission. So our trip is simply an experience. We returned to our hotel, ate our dinner, and started on our return trip up the river at 3:00 o'clock. At dusk, thinking we must be near the lake, we inquired of a man on the shore how far it was to Mullet lake. We were informed that we were about three miles up Black river. So we turned about, and when within about a mile of Cheybogan river, we started a camp where we are now sitting sociably around our camp fire and enjoying the grateful heat which these shingle culls and bolts throw out, lighting up in weird splendor the forest trees around us.

" 'Indian village on Burt's lake, October 27th. We left our camp at daybreak this morning and reached Mullet lake at about eight o'clock, where we lashed our canoes together, put

216

up our blanket sails, and scudded across the lake at a lively rate, reaching the portage between Mullet and Burt's lakes at noon. On looking over the land, we decided to haul our canoes across what we were given to understand was about a half a mile but which proved to be two miles, in order to save a trip of ten miles around the river. Accordingly, we drew the large one about half way and went back for the small one. This we took to where we had the other, hitching on to the large one again and took it across, arriving on the shore of Burt's lake at 8:00 o'clock in the evening where we were so tired that we decided to leave the other canoe in the woods. In some future day, some one in coming across the deserted canoe, will wonder how it came there.

" 'As our canoe would not carry all of us, two remain on the shore while four cross over to the Indian village. A kind Indian has allowed us to occupy his house, has given us our supper, and is preparing beds for our use for the night.

" 'Camp on Crooked lake, October 28th. We sent an Indian after the two who stayed on the east shore of the lake but he got lost in the fog and when he returned with them it was nearly noon. After dinner we started. Porter, Campbell and Dr. Fernside taking the trail, and the rest of us the canoe. We crossed Burt's lake to the mouth of the river connecting it with Crooked lake, and following its devious way through marsh and stream, we crossed Crooked lake to the shore north of the island (the present site of Odin) where we are preparing to camp for the night.

" 'Little Traverse, October 29th. After leaving our camp this morning, we experienced no difficulty until we struck the shallow stream connecting Crooked and Round lakes. This and Round lake we found so shallow, that we were obliged to wade and pull our empty canoe along. In order to keep our shoes and stockings dry, we took them off, and as a thin skim of ice had made during the night, the wading was anything put pleasant. We left our canoe on the west shore of Round lake, and walking about a half mile, we came to the shore of Little Traverse bay. A short walk along the beach brought us in sight of the Post-Boy. It was moored in a little nook by Porter and the doctor who had already arrived. As a lively breeze sprung up from the southwest, we were obligated to run for the harbor where we awaited the coming of a fair wind to start homeward.

" 'Old Mission, October 30th. We left Little Traverse harbor at midnight with a fair wind and, wing and wing, we sped along over the white capped waves, arriving at Old Mission dock at 10:00 o'clock this forenoon, in time to miss the snow storm that is just coming on.'

"I give an account of this trip as an instance of how difficult it was in those days to get from place to place, and comparing it then and now as called the 'Inland Route.' There are several villages on the shores of these lakes now, and a trip on one of the little steamers that traverse the lakes and rivers between Oden on Crooked lake and Cheybogan, is considered one of the most pleasant of this region."

Chapter XVIII

DOCTOR, LAWYER, MERCHANT, INVENTOR

No more detailed account has ever been written of the transition from the "old country" to the "new country" than this one by William Holdsworth.

Not highly educated by today's standards, Holdsworth must have surely been a near genius. His versatility, his skill in meeting challenge, and his devotion to his family, made him typical of the pioneer stock which built the Midwest.

The memoirs, which ended before the turn of the century, have been made available by Robert Holdsworth of East Dennis, Massachusetts, a grandson of William Holdsworth, artist, doctor, merchant, artisan, and, above all, pioneer.

"I was born on the 15th day of June, 1816, on Union street in the parish of St. George in East London.

"At an early age my parents moved to Tarling street near Commercial road.

"When about five years of age I was sent to a school kept by a widowed lady. After two years I was then sent to a boys school where I learned to write on a slate.

"When nine years old I was sent to Mr. Mathew Finley's academy where I studied arithmetic, mensuration, practical geometry, writing, ornamental writing, and bookkeeping, and became acquainted with Miss Lucy Finley who afterwards became French governess in the family of General Mawuveff in St. Petersburg.

"I was 11 when my father wished me to visit his brother who lived at Yoxford in Suffolk, so he started me off by four horse stage from the Bull Inn, Aldgate. The distance was over

100 miles, and they changed horses every 10 miles. One place where they changed horses, and where we had dinner, was the White Horse at Ipswich which is mentioned by Dickens in the Pickwick papers.

"My friends met me at Yoxford where I stayed about two weeks visiting and having a good time with the Miller's daughters (they were neighbors). After visiting around I returned by the same route to London.

"I remained at Mr. Finley's academy until 14 when I left to go into the employment of the London Dock Company as check clerk in the sugar department.

"One morning before office hours, one of the clerks (we used to call him Little Jimmy Green) was fishing on the quay of the dock and fell in. I heard him call out and found him afloat in the water. There were some sailors laughing at him. I jumped down into a barge and got him out. He had to go to Tower Hill, nearly a mile and a half, where he lived to change his clothes and then back to the office. Several years after, I went with some friends to visit the warehouses and wine vaults and there found Little Jimmy a grown up gentleman at a salary of $1600 a year.

"One morning, June 28, 1830, there was great trumpet blowing. When we boys got on the top of the warehouse and near the walls we saw a Herald trumpeter and suite. He was proclaiming the death of George the Fourth and the accession to the throne of William the Fourth.

"Another circumstance happened, not easily forgotten. One day we heard the Marine band playing the Death March. We went on the bridge in the docks which was parallel to a bridge on the street. We saw, following the band, a cart drawn by a horse. On the cart was a man sitting on a coffin who was being taken to Execution Dock on the bank of the river to be hung on a scaffold and remain until the tide rose to his feet, when he was to be cut down and given to his friends for burial. He had been convicted of piracy on the high seas and the penalty death by hanging. His name was Captain Davis.

"About this time my uncle died and this time I started from London bridge by the Hull steamer. When opposite Southwold on the coast of Suffolk they made a signal and the pilot boat came out and took me ashore. It was quite rough and I was quite seasick but as soon as I got ashore I was all right. I there met my aunt who greeted me kindly. We then rode to Yoxford after the funeral. I stayed several days and then returned by the same route to London bridge.

"When I neared the age of 15, June 15, 1831, my father thought I ought to learn a trade. He tried to get me apprenticed in the city of London but the premium was beyond his means so he apprenticed me to Richard Sanders of Leigh street, Burton Crescent, for six years or until I was 21. He paid a premium of 30 guineas.

"There I met with several occurrences which I will mention. We did work for Sir James Pollock, the Duke of Devonshire, and several of the nobility. Also for John J. Griffin, the father of Lady Franklin, who, with Sir John Franklin, I afterward met and assisted to fix his furniture on board the Farilie in the autumn of 1836 when he went to Van Dieman's Land as governor. Sir John left many books which the servants were burning when I saved a copy of Tom Paine's works and a copy of the poems of Thomas Gray.

"Soon after I went to Sanders' I was sent to collect a debt for a funeral of a child of Douglas William Jerrold's. I called upon the great novelist and he said he was too poor to pay then but did so afterwards.

"On the first of August, 1831, we were invited to visit the chambers of Sir Frederick Pollock to see the procession on the Thames of William the Fourth and the Queen, to open the new London bridge. I was too sick to attend. On the 5th of April, 1832, one of the men in our employ, who was also a scene shifter at Convent garden theatre, asked me if I would like to go on the stage and see the first performance of the Hunchback. I accepted the offer and put on a flannel jacket and an apron and went with him and got in as a scene shifter. I was stationed in the flies and

223

saw a grand sight, Helen Faucet as Julia, Sheridan Knowles as the Hunchback, and Miss Taylor as Helen. This was the first appearance of Helen Faucet and of the play. It was a grand sight to see the performance and the immense audience gathered to see it.

"On another evening I saw Madam Malibran in Sonambula. I soon entered the Mechanics Institution and attended the drawing classes and lectures, and at the Sovics met many celebrities of the period, Dr. Brickbeek, Lord Brougham, Miss Harriet Martineau, and her brother, R. H. Haydon, the artist, whose lectures and classes I attended.

"On the 16th of October, 1834, while visiting Mary Sanders in Doughty street, I heard a great outcry of fire which proceeded from a crowd of people who were rushing along the street and, upon inquiring where the fire was, discovered that the Houses of Parliament were on fire. I then followed the crowd along Holborn and Long Acre to the Strand and to Charring Cross, then along Parliament street where I saw the buildings on fire.

"On the 8th of March, 1835, which was Sunday, I met, by appointment, at 6:00 A.M. the young lady Mary Sanders. We walked to Holloway where we rested near Whittington's Stone, then proceeded to Holloway church (St. John's, Islington) where we were married in presence of our two friends, Mrs. Charles Thomson and Miss Hannah Read who were there as witnesses by appointment.

"On the 20th of June, 1837, while on my way home from the Institute and in front of the Royal Exchange I saw a large crowd and the Herald proclaiming the accession of Victoria to the throne.

"On July 24, I was at the home of my parents, where I was then living, when I saw a large balloon with a parachute attached which had started from Vauxhall Gardens. It was then nearing the place of descent which was Greenwich Park where the parachute was detached from the balloon and in its descent collapsed. The occupant, Mr. Cocking, was killed in Greenwich Park.

"On January 10, 1838, being Wednesday, I was on my way home from the Institute when nearing the Royal Exchange I saw it on fire and the Chimes were playing 'There's No Luck About the House.'

"On the 30th of October, 1841, the great fire of the Tower of London took place and I saw the ruins when I passed over Tower hill upon my visit to St. Thomas' hospital to see my mother who had undergone an operation and who died a few days afterward and was buried in the vaults of the Ebenezer Chapel, St. Georges in the East.

"After my apprenticeship I worked for a short period for Sir James McIntosh, the contractor, then went to work for the London Dock Company in the Engineers department. There I made the patterns for an air pump for the diving bell and the patterns for a 25 horse condensing engine. While working on some new lock gates, I had a visit from my late master, Richard Sanders, who had been visited by Mr. Hugh Biers, a large builder, who wished to employ a young man as Clerk of Works, inquiring about my ability to fill that position. He was satisfied with his recommendation and I was at once engaged to fill that office. During this time I had to make the working drawings and superintend the construction of large villa buildings extending along the Maida Vale road three-fourths of a mile to Kilburn Gate. A stack of 12 store buildings and a large hotel building were included in the distance.

"While there for some time, I occupied an old farm house called Bone Farm said to have been occupied by Gay, the poet, where he wrote the Beggars Opera. Here some of our children were born. During this period I became acquainted with several of the purchasers of the villas, Sir John Ross, the arctic discoverer; Mr. Cooper, the tragedian; Mr. Greisbach, the composer; Mr. Spiers, and others. On completing the store building I rented one of them and commenced business in the plumbing, painting, and glazing line. I also built two villas in St. John's Wood.

"During this time I met with several losses in bad debts and was obliged to relinquish business.

225

"While with Biers, who was an auctioneer and valuer, I was called upon to value some machinery for cutting sheet cork invented by an American. It cut sheets as thin as bank note paper. I had several sheets and had an idea that they would make good hats. I made one and showed it to Mr. Spiers who was in that business in the city. In a few days I found that a patent had been taken for cork hats, but not as my invention but the party I had shown it to who reaped the benefit.

"Being out of business, I accepted a position in a steam saw mill and while there I answered an advertisement for an assistant engineer and got the position with Elija Galloway of Buckingham street in the Strand. There I was called upon to visit the office of the public sewers and find the depths of the sewers in various parts of London for the purpose of the underground railways 1844 and 1845. In 1846, during the great railway rage, I was employed to take the levels for the Nottingham, Birmingham, and Coventry Junction and the Chelmsford and Malden railways. The levels were taken under great opposition from the owners of lands. The plans and sections had to be deposited by the 30th of November. Had several assistants employed to get the work done in time. I worked day and night superintending the work without rest for six days and nights and at the end found the directors had failed to comply with the necessary qualifications.

"After the collapse of the railway mania, Elija Galloway turned his attention to improvements in railway engines and construction in which I assisted. He was a most prolific thinker and inventor but unfortunately a bad drinker, was for days unfit for business, had a young and beautiful wife who was also addicted to the same habits and of whom he was awfully jealous. He and, the parties connected with him, hired one side of the Hungerford market and there erected a model railway at an incline of 30 degrees on which a model locomotive was run up the incline, it was worked by compressed air and carried me up a distance of 200 feet. We had several distinguished visitors, Sir

226

John Rennie, Lord Oakney, Captain Fitzmaurice, and many others.

"At this time a side track on the Great Western railway on a steep incline at Taplow near Maidenhead was secured, also a locomotive which was altered and used for the purpose, the construction of which I superintended. While riding with the engine driver on one of the Great Western engines which I frequently did on my returns to London, I had an idea of an atmospheric brake, a sketch of which I made in my leveling book but as I afterwards met with an accident, which I will not relate, I forgot all about it.

"A day was appointed for the experiment, the 29th of January, 1849. The locomotive was attached to a wire rope to be lowered by a windlass or crab. While being lowered, I stood on the side of the track with a crowbar in my hand. In the act of lowering the engine the rope broke, Galloway sang out 'For God's sake thrust in the bar.' In doing so it slipped and came around on the wheel, striking me on the head, and the rope trailing behind coiled up around me and I was carried down the embankment in and out of a hawthorne hedge for a distance of one hundred yards. On being picked up, there was part of the hedge fixed on my face. Thinking I was dead, I was taken to the Dumb Bell Inn at Taplow. On examination my thigh was found broken, also one of my collar bones. Three physicians attended me, one from London and two from the neighborhood. After being unconscious for 36 hours I came to and my thigh was set and my shoulder bandaged and a nurse was attending me. My wife was there but soon returned to London. She came every few days to see me. I laid there eleven weeks on my back.

"At this time my father died and I was unable to attend his funeral. He was buried in the churchyard of St. Georges in the East.

"When I was able to get about on crutches I came to London. I was unable to get any employment for eleven months, then I was recommended to Mr. James Edwards as bookkeeper where I remained nine years.

227

"Soon after I went to Edwards, there was a detachment of hussars quartered at the stables and a great meeting of special constables at Davis's riding school near-by. Among them was Louis Napoleon who was one of the sworn contables and afterwards Emperor of the French. The occasion was the supposed Charles' rising which never took place.

"About this time I saw a store to rent in Middle Row, Knightsbridge, which I hired and started an 'Artists Repository' for the sale of artists' materials. I was acquainted with the store keeper at the Kensington Museum and got an order for some drawing boards and squares and drawing models which I commenced manufacturing in a workshop adjoining.

"I had a customer, Mr. Corbould, teacher of drawing to the Princess Royal and the young Princes. The Prince of Wales and Duke of Edinburg visited the store and purchased some drawing pencils and other things. Mr. Corbould gave me an order for a large drawing pad for the Princess Royal which I had made and covered with purple silk. When I took it to the palace and sent it up to her she sent word down wishing to know whether she kept an elephant to carry it about for her, it being built as a quarto elephant block. I had to take it back and furnish a smaller one.

"I furnished the schools at South Kensington and the art schools in the country with human skeletons and stand encircled with curtains for drawing purposes. I became acquainted with Professor Huxley of the geological museum in Jermyn street and furnished him with several anatomical specimens of snakes, frogs, birds, and animals which came to me from Paris. One day he received me to send to the Zoological Gardens Regents Park for a tortoise which he wished to be skeletonized and mounted. I sent a young man with a bag for it not knowing how large it was. The keeper of the gardens asked him what conveyance he had brought for it. He did not tell him but had to procure a horse and cart for the purpose as it was the large tortoise which had been carrying children on its back about the gardens. It was over 100 years old. I had it taken to the Anatomical School of St. Georges Hospital and had it put in the pickling vat on the roof where it remained about three weeks and became a perfect skeleton. Then I had it articulated and mounted and sent to the museum.

"At this time the Crystal Palace in Hyde Park was in course of construction and every Sunday visited the park to see its progress. Upon its completion and on the first of May, 1851, knowing a friend whose house abutted on the park we went there and saw the Queen Victoria and Prince Albert escorted by the Horse Guards, Louis Napoleon, Emperor of the French, and many of the nobility proceeding to open the palace. I visited the palace several times.

"Being acquainted with a member of the Guards Club, he loaned me his Ivory which admitted me to the opera. I went one evening in full dress and saw and heard Madam Grisi as Sappho, passed several of Edwards' customers there who, of course, did not know me. I afterwards visited Madam Grisi and Signior Mario at their villa at Brompton when they gave me a cheque for the hire of their carriage horses which we supplied.

"Having forgotten several occurrances in the proper order, I will not relate them.

"In 1830 my cousin, William Watson, was in the employ of the East India Company and sailed on one of their ships, the London. He took me on board to show me over the vessel. The company's vessels were fitted as warships and carried large crews. When any of the crew died they employed six Chinamen to fill the place of each one, so there were on most voyages a large number of Chinamen employed.

"He took me between the decks where the Chinamen were. All around they were squatted playing games but most of them gambling for pice, a round coin with a square hole in the center. Others were eating rice with chop sticks, but all were busy.

"My cousin brought me some Chinese colors and India ink and brushes fixed in thin bamboo strips with covers of the same to protect the points. He also brought us jars of preserved ginger, mangoes, and crepe shawls for mother and sister.

"The Admiralty sessions at the Old Bailey being in progress and a captain of a vessel being tried for piracy, he took me to hear it. It was a very exciting trial but the man was acquitted. As soon as the verdict of the jury was announced the man placed his hands on the front of the dock and leaped to meet his friends who were waiting to hear the results and the audience applauded.

"After several voyages my cousin settled at the Cape of Good Hope and opened a hotel.

"In the east of London at that time the East India Company had a large building where they kept the Chinamen during their stay, as they were obliged to return them to China. One day they had a great procession with bands of music, tom-toms, fifes, etc., carrying several idols and proceeded to the Regents canal where, with great ceremony, they threw the idols into the water, then returned in procession to the building.

"In 1832 while at Sanders', who was an undertaker as well as builder, we had a funeral to attend. It was to be somewhat out of the ordinary, being that of a woman who had kept a house of assignation. There was to be a hearse and four with feathers and six mourning coaches and pairs. As there were few mourners I was deputed to ride in one of the coaches. When the hearse began to move from the house there was a great hooting and yelling from the crowd as she was a noted bad character. No expense was spared on the funeral by the man said to be her husband. She was buried at St. Giles in the fields. The house was near the one in Kingsgate street, Holborn, where Sarah Camp lived, mentioned by Charles Dickens in Martin Chuzzlewit.

"As Sanders was too high-toned to attend an Irish funeral I was deputed once to attend one. It was along Seymour street, Custon Square, they stopped in front of a gin shop and wanted to know if I had any objection to going in with them to have a drink. I objected as far as myself was concerned but they might do as they pleased. They did and I waited outside. When they had their wish they came out and we proceeded on our return to the house that had been one of mourning.

"In 1838 I had an offer to go to South Australia for the South Australian Company at Adelaide but had to decline it as I was then in employ.

"In 1849 I had an offer to go to Spain on railway business. Also one from an East Indian railway but being lame I had to decline.

"The various dates I forgot but I saw the following at Drury Lane theatre. Mr. Cooper as Massionella at the Haymarket, Mr. McReady as Hamlet at the Adelphi, Paul Bedford as Blueskins, Mr. and Mrs. Keely and Mr. and Mrs. Florence in the American Cousins at Drury Lane; and also Charles Matthews at the Great Magician.

"Went to Vauxhall gardens and saw the siege of Sebastapol, also visited the Crystal Palace at Sydenham and at Greenwich Hospital saw the hall painted by Sir James Thornhill, the picture gallery at Dulwich, the National Gallery, and the British Museum. I called at St. James' palace to see the Marchioness of Westmeath who wished me to sell her carriage, which I did, and she gave me five pounds. Also saw, on business, Lord Chesterfield, Lord Mahon, Sir Henry Bulwer, Lord Lofters, and many others of the nobility. I saw the funeral of the Duke of Sussex at Kensal Green Cemetery and the Duke of Wellington at Hyde Park Corner. Visited Tattersalls where I purchased, on commission, some noted hounds for Mr. Kennedy, the Commissioner of Woods and Forests.

"Went to a dinner given by the Duchess of Kent to her trades people, I representing the firm for which I was bookkeeper. We had venison and game and everything in season sent by the Duchess. As we were postmasters to the queen and Royal family we supplied them with post horses to the different railway stations. On the Derby days we were kept busy from 4:00 o'clock in the morning, started 20 pairs and fours with drags for the races, post boys with satin jackets and caps and large bouquets, also grand turnouts for weddings.

"In 1857, both members of the firm being dead, the business was closed about this time, my contract with the South Kensington Museum having expired, the firm of Cubit having taken it at a lower price and my business not being sufficient for a living and my family. I thought it advisable to immigrate to the United States, where I had a sister. I sold my business, packed up my machinery and goods and started for Liverpool on the 25th of August, 1858.

"We went on board the clipper ship Charlotte A. Stamler for Quebec and sailed the next day. Had a good trip through the Irish sea but when we arrived at Cork the sea was rougher and most of us became seasick. After a few days we were near the Bay of Biscay and the weather still kept stormy but occasionally cleared up with some fine days. One day being rather rough and being on deck, the baby, Will S., kept rolling from one side of the ship to the other; he was two years and eight months old. We had some nice folks, passengers from Sheffield and other places, had music, singing, and games on fine days. We saw whales spouting, porpoise rolling and jumping, and sharks occasionally, some beautiful sunsets and risings.

"Early in October we made the Gulf of St. Lawrence, came up the river and arrived at Quebec the 5th of October, 1858. We landed at Quebec, passed goods at Custom house, then went by train on the Grand Trunk to Montreal, thence to Toronto where we stopped at a druggist's and got the medicine chest filled up and provisions for the remainder of the journey, stopped at Collingwood one night and day and moved our goods onto the propeller Hunter and started for Northport, Michigan.

"We went through the Georgian Bay and landed at Mackinaw Island for wood, then the next place we made was Pickard's dock at Northport where we landed our goods. Then we went across to Northport to find someone to take our goods to the Mission-peninsula. We found Captain Joe Dearwood and engaged him for the trip next day. As he could not sail that day we engaged Captain Mason to take us and our bedding to our destination.

"About six o'clock it began to get dark so we made for Tucker's point where we landed for the night. It began to rain hard but we managed to make a tent with our sheets and with brush we started a good fire, Captain Mason doing the work with all of us helping we kept up a good fire and covered up with bedding and remained until daylight. We then went across the point and found we were within a few rods of Mormon Preacher Tucker's house. We then went back to the boat, got our blankets and sheets aboard and started for the peninsula, passed the island, following the shore where we could see a brush fire, and late in the day we landed at Hopkins. It was the 13th of October, 1858.

"We counted heads and found the family as follows: self, 42; wife, Mary S. 46; Mary Elizabeth 20; John 15; Henry 13; Peregrine 11; Clementina 8; Fanny 6; and Will S. 2 years and 8 months.

"My sister and her husband were glad to see us, but as their house was very small they would do the best to make us comfortable. We got our bedding ashore and after supper fixed up for the night. It was an awful cold one. In the morning we found ice half an inch thick in the room. Thought we had got to a cold country.

"After a good breakfast we began to think what had best be done. First, to find where we could get some land, so I, with one of the boys, started for the village of Traverse City and found out where the land office was, it being then in the court house standing where the present court house is. I introduced myself to Jacob Barnes who was then the registrar, looked over the plot book and found that lot 2, section 24, 27N 11W was on the market being next north of Robert Hopkins and containing 30 acres for the price of $37.50 in gold. I paid the cash in English sovereigns and got a certificate of purchase. Then found the county clerk, Theron Bostwick, and declared my intention to become a citizen of the United Seates and got my first papers for that purpose.

"After that we looked about and found the store of 'The Company' which at that time was on the north side of the river. I introduced myself to Henry D. Campbell who was known as 'Big Henry.' I bought some pork and flour and groceries and packed them back to the peninsula along the trail made by the Indians, partly by the banks of the bay.

"Our next thing was to locate a place for the house and clean it up. When we got back we found Joe Dearwood had arrived with our machinery and goods and got them ashore. The water was much higher than now, being nearly four feet higher and running up to where the fish shanty now is. The goods being all packed in cases, lined with tin, they remained on the shore until we had a place built to stow them.

"The next day we selected a place for the house about six rods north of the south line and commenced clearing a spot for the house and outbuildings. The following day we went to town with John and Henry to the lumber yard near the mill, bought 3,000 feet of lumber, made a raft along side the dock, bought a long line and fixed to the raft, got some long poles, then started the raft, John helping me to pole it along and Henry to pull the rope along the shore of the bay. We started about 6:00 P.M. and about midnight arrived at our destination, fortunately the bay was calm and we beached the raft and tied it up to a tree until the morning when we carried the lumber to the place for the house. We then dug a pit, or cellar, and boarded it up for stowing potatoes, 100 bushels which we had purchased from the Squire, a neighbor by the name of Langworthy, at 30 cents a bushel, the greatest number of varieties I ever saw before or since, or all colors and sizes which I presume he had got from Indiana. I only got 50 bushels at first and the balance at sundry times.

"Now having several callers, we made arrangement for a raising bee which was to be the 5th of November when the following neighbors assembled: Joe Hesler, John McMullen, Louis Clement, Harvey Langworthy, Bill Buchan, Frank and Curtis Fowler, and Pat Carmody. They brought two span of oxen for hauling and raising the logs and then the work began. They made good progress and at noon we all assembled to enjoy a good dinner, prepared by my wife who was a first rate cook.

"After dinner the work proceeded until about dusk when it began to snow, we then were ready for the roof. The next day some of the men came again and put up the rafters, and the boys and myself covered the roof with two thicknesses of boards. We laid the floors and put up the partitions. We also built an addition on the south side of the house for a kitchen and store room. We went up to town to buy a cook stove and a box stove to keep the house warm as it was now freezing nights and very cold days. We also had to get windows but the doors we made. I could not get glabed sashes as they did not keep them for sale. I had to unglaze some and buy the glass, those that were too large I had to cut to fit. That I did easily as I had brought a glazier's diamond with me; the putty I had to make and glazed the sash, hung the doors and made the house quite comfortable.

"I bought a cow and built a shed for her and as Mary was a good milker we had plenty of milk, cream, and butter. Bought some chickens of the Squire and had eggs. Had to get hay from the neighbors and feed from the store. We also had to get some axes and we then commenced clearing.

"Not having had experience in cutting down trees, I found it very hard work, some of them being quite large; one about four feet took us nearly a day to get down. As we were prepared with cross cut saw and other tools and knew how to use them we made good progress. We sawed up the logs in lengths we could handle, trimmed off the limbs and piled them up in small heaps. Kept up good fires with dead wood and brush during the winter and in the spring of 1859 I had nearly four acres cleared and partly logged.

"In the meantime I let a job to John Logan to clear up eight acres. He brought an ox team and cleared up the balance of our chopping, making together about 12 acres and piled the brush, burning what we could; the balance was burned in the spring.

235

"In June we found snow and ice under the piles of brush. Cleared up the whole, ready for crops, the eight acres ready for sowing spring wheat.

"During this time our neighbor, Joe Hestler, had a sugar bush and was commencing to make sugar. We helped him carry the sap and attend fires at night, boiling the sap and had in the spring 80 pounds of sugar and several gallons of molasses.

"It was now early May and the ground ready for sowing; the next thing was to get seed wheat; none was to be had in the neighborhood, so we hired Joe Hestler's boat in the East bay and Henry and myself rowed to the Old Mission and bought 16 bushels of spring wheat of Mr. Enoch Waite for $3.00 a bushel. Got it hauled over after bringing it up in the boat and on the 22nd of May, 1859, John Logan sowed it and in the fall had it cut. When thrashed we found it produced 22 bushels to the acre, the best crop of wheat I ever raised. After using what we needed for flour and seed, sold the balance for $3.00 a bushel.

"Spring arrived and we had some land plowed and commenced making a garden. We brought seeds with us and during the summer raised all the vegetables we needed for the family, the cow, pigs, and chickens.

"In addition to the cow shed, I built a pen for the pigs, a couple of which I bought from Mr. Carmody.

"A number of visitors now called, among them were Mr. and Mrs. Hannah and the baby Julius, also Mr. Dunlap who was then looking for land and afterwards located on the opposite shore at Bingham. The Indians often visited us. There were Pewash and Coggy and several others. They would sometimes wish to sleep in the stable and often would bring a jug with them, the contents of which they obtained at Squire Bryant's, justice of the peace, who dealt in fire water. They would go to sleep for the night, not annoying us in the least. We were always on good terms with the Indians who afterwards worked for me loading wood on the scows and vessels.

"We now set to work preparing for threshing the wheat. I rigged up a small horizontal windwill with gearing and built a thrashing machine. After we had rigged our machine we had several callers, among them Anthony and Joseph Greilick and others, to see the rig. After the wheat was cut and hauled we commenced thrashing which we soon accomplished by our windmill gearing. Then we winnowed most of it by hand and the wind and sieves which we made by punching holes in sheets of tin nailed on wooden frames and shook by connecting with the machinery.

"On the 10th of October, 1858, we were surprised by a call from Captain Fred Johnson who came up to the landing in a boat and then to the house. He wished to know whether I would go with him to the Harbor to see Colonel Bowers who was very sick with a stoppage of his bowels. He had learned that I had a medicine chest. It was a clear but very cold night. We took the medicine and got on board the boat and started on the trip. The Captain rowed and I steered and after a long pull made the island. It was a fine moonlight night, the moon being at full. We fastened the boat and went on shore where we fortunately found some fire left by the government surveyors. Got some dry wood and made a good blaze, well warmed up and started for the opposite shore where Colonel Bowers lived. I found him quite sick. Dr. Shetterly had been attending him a week without any favorable result. His remedies had been mostly external with some herbal internal remedies. I mixed him some active mineral powders which I gave him. Remained with him during the night and before morning had procured a passage. Left some powders and returned by the same route. The folks were much pleased with the result and they gave me the credit for saving his life.

"My daughter, Mary Elizabeth, taught school at the Harbor and occasionally boarded there, the custom then was for the teacher to board around and to be paid by a rate bill collected by the assessor of the district.

"The winter of 1859 kept us all busy clearing up and burning brush and looking after the livestock. We now had a cow and calf and some young pigs. Got some grass seed and sowed it. The

237

cow browsed in the woods, also the pigs lived a great deal on beechnuts which were plentiful.

"As summer approached and having brought with us a pair of dissolving view lanterns and sheet for exhibiting, together with several foreign views and moving figures, and a large microscope and slides to be lighted by an Oxycalcium light. The gas bag I had with me, I made some oxygen gas and limeballs. I bought, from Captain Dearwood, a skiff with centerboard, sail, and oars, and was then ready for a start, got everything on board. John, Henry, and myself sailed around Mission Point and arrived safe at Elk Rapids. We exhibited in a large room at the hotel and had a good audience. John played the accordian and Henry helped me to exhibit. Showed the various views and moving figures. Then the Oxycalcium microscope and slides gave a good exhibition which was very successful and we took in several dollars which at that time was very acceptable as the funds were getting low. We then, in the early morning, started back and sailed and rowed to the New Mission. After seeing Mr. Dougherty and Lewis Miller, they thought they could not raise enough funds to show there. We started back on our homeward trip where we arrived on the following day after starting.

"When we came back we found that, the night before, the folks had been scared soon after dark by hearing the pigs squealing and making a great noise, so they got William Hopkins to go with them and, taking a lantern and a gun, they went out and found one of the large pigs had been killed by some animal and thought it was a bear. They looked around but did not see anything so they thought it best to leave it until morning. Soon after daylight they went out again and found the pig had gone so they hunted for it and found it had been removed and partly eaten, the work of a bear which was afterwards seen by Joe Hestler and afterwards killed by John Warren who was a great hunter. He also killed a deer in a place they called Woodchuck Hollow lying between, at that time Mr. Carmody's, now Adams's, and Wilsons'.

238

"The fall now coming on I found the boys were able to manage the farm and livestock so I started for town at the head of the bay to get a job for the winter. I saw McKillip who was the boss and he wanted to know what I could do. I told him any rough carpenters work or measuring logs. He did not think much of me but he said I could go up in the camps. I stayed at the boarding house that night and went with the supply team in the morning. On November 25, 1859, started for the camp, went east along what is now Traverse City, then along the road and past the boarding house and store kept by John Black. Thence along through the swamp, then turned south and along the dugway. Here we had to get out and walk up the hill. Arriving at the top, we again got up and rode. Stopped and had some lunch on the road and arrived at the camp about dusk. Unpacked and got the fires lighted and the bunks fixed up, the bedding got in and ready for the night. The teamsters got the horses and mules fixed up in the stables. The cook had supper ready and the men set to and got their fill, and then were ready for bed. We turned into the bunks and were soon asleep for the night.

"Next day we had to fix up the sleighs ready for the woods. The men fixed up their axes and started for work. I had then to go to the rollway and fix up a place to keep my book and log rule and was then ready for the first load of logs to start the winter's cut. It was, to me, the beginning of a new life and it kept me busy to keep warm and scale the logs as they came along on the sleds, the teamsters vieing with each other to see who could haul the biggest loads.

"I soon got used to it and the teamsters wanted the logs to be fully scaled but I started on the square as I wanted the winter's cut to hold out at the mills. The men being away from the camp some distance took their dinners with them or had it sent by the chore boy with some hot coffee. The boarding house was near the rollway and I got dinner there.

"It was an exciting time when the boys (men are boys when in the camps) came from the woods, washing and combing and getting ready for supper that was always ready for them. After supper the fun began, playing cards, dominoes and other games. I had come prepared for business, having brought with me copybooks and paper, pens and ink; I canvassed the crew to see if any of them wished to improve themselves in writing. The following accepted the offer: George Evans, L. Swaney, J. Traverse, George Cutler, P. Peters, G. Miller, R. Young, Jim Feeley, W. Williams, Dutch Carpenter, Paul Rider, Brown C. Stafford, and Ole Oleson. Everything went pleasantly.

"The time book and the amount of logs put in the river were sent to town weekly, the teams going up one day and down the next, everything being done in a business manner.

"It was nearing Christmas. I found John Logan, who was in the adjoining camp, and we arranged to start on Saturday, the day before Christmas about 4:00 P.M. We had to walk 26 miles so it was pretty late before we got home. We spent Christmas day each at our homes. In the afternoon we met and walked back to the camps ready for the next week's work. The winter passed very pleasantly.

"During the fall of 1859 and the early winter of 1860 the Company had constructed a building for a new store (part of which was later held by Caldwell and Loudon). They had also bought, in Chicago, the propeller Alleghany which arrived on May 1st, 1860; Mr. and Mrs. Leach were passengers. On the next day, May second, the men came down from the camps and on the following day the boat went out, 62 men going out from the camps. John went out to work for the Illinois Central Railroad. After going home and seeing everything was going all right I packed up some tools and went to work for the Company.

"I took a job for Perry Hannah to fill the mortice wheels at the old grist mill in Slab City (then called Bagdad) which was then run by water power and was managed by Mr. Shilson.

"The frame of a new store had been put up by J. K. Pymton, Sib Dame and others, and was then ready for fitting. Victor Petertyl made the sash of cherry and I made the front sash doors of pine. Sib Dame, Petertyl, and I did the inside fittings under the direction of Mr. Smith Barnes of Port Huron, who

240

came about this time and the store was opened and the goods from the old store moved in and new goods brought in from Chicago on the Alleghany. Most of this work was done for $16 a month.

"I now took some work by the piece because I thought I could earn more that way. I took a job to lathe the two rooms for offices and the passage for $17 and wrote 617 letters for which I got one cent a letter. I did the latter job in less than two days. The wheels I did in less than a week for which I got $8.

"I was then making too much money so Perry Hannah charged me for my board. While working by the day, I was found board. When Mr. Gill, the plasterer, came to do the plastering, he was mad because I had done the lathing. I thought he would not do it but soon altered his mind.

"Mrs. Hannah wanted her rooms papered and wished to know whether I could do it. I agreed. When I commenced trimming the paper she wished to know if she could not help. I declined. Then when I was making the paste, she wanted to know if I did not put glue in it, said Sib Dame did. I said I could make good paste that would stick without glue and when the job was done she was much pleased. About this time I papered some rooms for J. F. Grant, the bookkeeper.

"Then I made some patterns for a new gang saw for Thomas Cutler for the new mill and made a pinion pattern, for the both I got $32.50. I then went for awhile before going to the camp for the winter.

"On the 14th of September, 1860, the propeller Lady Elgin was sunk in Lake Michigan and 400 lives lost.

"John came in by the Alleghany and went to work in the camps and Mary Elizabeth went out to Mr. Say's to look after the children after finishing her school at the Harbor.

"On the 13th of December, 1860, I went to McRae's camp in the pineries and remained there until I received the following characteristic letter dated January 8th, 1861:

241

'Traverse City
January 8, 1861

'Mr. Wm. Holdsworth
'Dear Sir:
    'We are thinking of employing some person here that we can use as an assistant to Mr. Grant in writing a portion of the time, and the balance do something else. What portion of the time would be in the office I am not now able to say, but perhaps 2 to 3 days per week. I thought that the situation might be such a one as you would like — the payments not be more than you are now getting, at least until we made you more useful. You will understand that the books will be in charge of Mr. Grant and your position would be to do what he might wish you in writing up pass books, etc. and such other writing as we may wish.
    'Mr. Grant and yourself would both be under the direction of Mr. Barnes so far as he shall wish to command in all the business in the office of whatever nature.
    'When not employed in the office I think we would find you business at your trade — it is possible that the time may not be far distant when all your time would be required in writing.
    'You may write me your mind by the return trip and I will then determine what we do.

                              Yours,
                              [signed] Perry Hannah'

    "I took the position Mr. Hannah offered.
    "March 26, there was a great cry of fire and rushing out I found the court house was on fire. My large camera and photographic apparatus were in the building but I was too late to save them. The land office books and most of the county books were saved, being thrown out of the window. But all my things were gone and I never found the least trace of them. Bostwick said he lost over a hundred dollars in gold and I never heard that he ever found any of it. The fire and sand swallowed it up. I had just put out my shingle and was getting ready to take

pictures, my camera would take pictures 8 inches x 10 inches, and the whole was worth $120.00 and was a great loss to me, but, at this time a great deal of my time was employed at the store.

"April 12, 1861, war at the south began with the firing on Fort Sumter. May 31, H. D. Campbell was appointed postmaster with his office at Bagdad. June 3, Stephen Douglas died. June 14, Jacob Barnes left and Morgan Bates appointed in his place. June 20, 1861, George Richardson came and preempted 80 acres at the east of Hopkins clearing and Henry and Peregrine commenced chopping. When William Hopkins tried to prevent them, he could not, so applied to Mr. Bryant who said he had no authority.

"After some time George could find nothing to do at his trade so he went to New York and abandoned his claim. Hopkins then preempted it and now holds it.

"August 2, three boys drowned in the bay, Sedgwick Stevens and two Green boys, the sons of Michael Green who had his leg broken at that time in the sawmill.

"August 30, Mrs. Frankenberg and Paul Riter were tried for the murder of Nick Frankenberg and acquitted but no doubt of their guilt. Paul Riter went to Chicago by the boat previously and it was supposed bought arsenic there but no proof could be obtained. September 22, John Hopper went shooting ducks at Mud lake and accidentally shot himself.

"October 6, the following men left for the war: Abe Adsit, James Nicholson, Ike Winnie, Ed Stanley, Dudley Waite, George Flack, Mat Shanly, John O'Leary, Ben Ratelle, Eben Stone, Pat Graham, George Askey, William Callison, John Rodart, Joseph Williams, Lewis Stevens, Giles Gibson, A. W. Anderson, Edward Bewaire, I. Avery, C. Avery, Francis Waite, and John Hopkins.

"December 6, Oscar A. Stevens went away and Reuben Goodrich was appointed in his place as receiver of the land office."

Chapter XIX

CENTURY NOTES
(NEWS OF 1866)

For a number of years "Century Notes" has been a weekly column on the editorial pages of the *Traverse City Record-Eagle*. In it has appeared scores of news notes of a century ago ...... un-edited, sometimes caustic, and staunchly Republican. The year 1866 was one of turmoil and unrest in the United States as political parties were born and died in infancy. This was that year.

★ ★ ★

"Tony Nelson, an old colored man, died near Suffolk, Virginia, and was buried on the fourth of this month, in the 94th year of his age. This old man was formerly a servant in the George Washington family, and helped to cut what is known as the 'Washington ditch,' a canal leading from the western margin of Dismal swamp to Drummond's lake, an enterprise which was projected by General Washington. Tony had never lived, during his life, two miles from the Dismal swamp, and most of his time in the swamp. He had been the husband of twenty-two wives, six of whom are now living, and yet, in his extreme old age and last sickness not one of them would nurse him."

★ ★ ★

"The dinner given to the President at Delmonico's in New York cost $25,000. The wines cost from $10 to $20 a bottle. We can't conceive how the President could make such a silly speech under the influence of such costly wine. It reads like three cent whiskey, and bad at that."

244

"The French Company which undertook the completion of the great Virginia canal from Richmond to the Ohio River, has failed, or abandoned the enterprise. The scheme, it is said, was originally projected, or backed, by Louis Napoleon, as a part of his American 'policy,' by which he was to convert the Southern Confederacy into a magnificent French colony. When the Confederacy 'went up the spout' the canal project followed it."

★ ★ ★

"A well known official of Cincinnati had his 'shirt' stolen during the trip up the river with the presidential party. He pulled the garment off on going to bed to prevent its being rumpled, and when he awoke the next morning found to his dismay that it had been stolen. He performed the balance of the trip with his coat buttoned close up to his chin."

★ ★ ★

"The *Nebraska City News* says a shower of minute insects visited that place on the 24th of last month. The *News* says: 'The air was filled with winged insects, resembling in their flight the blow of the cottonwood, borne by the winds of spring. When viewed in the rays of the sun, a heavy fall of snow seemed impending. The curious little insects were in two strata; the upper stratum passed in a direct course to the west, impelled by the stiff east wind which had been prevailing for some days. The lower layer was moving in every direction. Some of them would strike against the house sides, others again would sail towards the earth, as if with the purpose of alighting, but if any lit upon the ground they could only be seen while looking towards the sun.' "

★ ★ ★

"The St. Louis correspondent of the *Springfield* (Mass.) *Republican* published the following: 'Coming down Chestnut street one day last week, I was struck by the appearance of an old man past sixty, who wore a thread-bare coat, shiny with constant wear, and whose hat was bruised and seedy. His head was bent towards the earth and his walk was a tottering shuffle,

245

the effect of whiskey and old age. He reeled from one side of the pavement to the other, and at last brought up against a lamp post on the corner, when a young-looking loafer coming along saluted him with 'Hullo, Jim, come and take a drink?'

"The old man's eye brightened, and, arm in arm he sauntered along to the nearest grogery with his companion. Five years ago that old man was James Green, United States Senator from Missouri, and in the days of the Kansas and Lecompton matters he was, next to Stephen A. Douglas, the ablest debater in Congress. But the war broke out, Mr. Green was sent to the rebel Congress, soon lost his property, his position, and his character, and now he is a poor drunkard and earns barely a pitance of a living as a calaboose shyster.' "

★ ★ ★

"A new system of small coinage is now under consideration by the government, and will in all probability be adopted. The proposed new cent is to be made of nickel, the same as at present, but the center of the coin has a raised star, the nucleus of which is represented by a hole through the coin. The two cent pieces have two perforated stars, and the three coins three. Thus, by holding either denomination to the light or by simply touching them so as to feel the holes, the value of a piece of money is unmistakably known. The half dime and dime are large coins, and of better metal, but are to be distinguished by one or two perforated stars."

★ ★ ★

"Brigham Young's daughter, Fannie, being strongly argued to accept a vulgar fraction of the hand and heart of one of her father's friends, agreed to the arrangement on condition that she should have as many husbands as the gentleman had wives. The man wouldn't consent and withdrew his suit."

★ ★ ★

"The latest thieving device is reported to be done in this way: A young man and a girl, both dressed to personate rural innocence as well as possible, enter a jewelry establishment and

246

bashfully ask to be shown some wedding rings. With much billing and cooing in the part of the young man, and a great show of modesty and coyness on that of the girl, the pair amuse the jeweler, while one or other or both secrete on their persons some of his stock and then leave."

★　★　★

"An expedition is now forming at St. Joseph, Missouri, to go to the gold mines of Arizona and Sonora, and will start from that city about the 20th of June. The company will be under the immediate command of Colonel McKinney, late of the United States Army, and will be under strict discipline. Each one will be armed with Spencer rifles and Colt's navies."

★　★　★

"An eight hour ordinance has been passed by the Detroit Common Council. The scale of prices for labor is as follows: Street laborers working ten hours a day get $1.65 per day, while those working eight hours get only $1.35. Man and team working ten hours get $3.75, eight hours, $3.

★　★　★

"The most extraordinary instance of patience on record in modern times is that of an Illinois judge, who listened silently for two days while a couple of wordy attorneys contended about the construction of an act of the legislature, and then ended the controversy by quietly remarking: 'Gentlemen, the law is repealed.' "

★　★　★

"A boy died in Chicago last week from the effects of swimming in a pond where the carcasses of animals had been deposited. Large spots broke out on him, and his symptoms were those of a very bad case of poisoning. It is supposed he swallowed some of the water."

★　★　★

"A murderous assault was made on Governor Fairchild of Wisconsin on the first of this month. While walking in his own

247

grounds, someone came on him from behind and struck him a heavy blow with a slingshot, which was so far evaded by the Governor's turning that the blow only grazed and bruised his forehead. He drew a pistol, which snapped when the ruffian fled. No clue has been discovered to the assailant and there is no explanation, except an anonymous letter from Washington some months ago stating that his life was threatened by a southerner."

★ ★ ★

"Cyrus W. Field, who has labored so indefatigably to secure the success of the Atlantic telegraph, recently returned from England, making his thirty-sixth voyage across the ocean on this enterprise. He returns to England to sail on the Great Eastern on its second attempt to lay the cable."

★ ★ ★

"Mrs. Lincoln has presented Fred Douglass with a cane of her husband's, carrying out a wish which the latter expressed shortly before his assassination."

★ ★ ★

"James Littleworth of Tennessee, now 78 years old, is the father of 31 children, the oldest of whom is fifty years old, and the youngest four months old. He is living with his fourth wife, whom he married at the age of fifty-nine, she being then a little Indian squaw of fourteen."

★ ★ ★

"A sloop, having 150 Negroes on board, was seized by a government vessel at Mobile on the 16th. These Negroes have been deluded to come from Nashville, Louisville, and Memphis by a promise of work at good wages but the parties in the transaction intended to take them to Cuba and sell them into slavery. The officers of the sloop are in custody."

★ ★ ★

"A curious revelation of the odd manner in which some of the 'gamins' of a great city live, was made in New York recently. A police officer in chase of some boys supposed to be thieves, traced them under one of the piers on the East river, where he found to his surprise that they were concealed in a house of their own building. The structure fifteen feet long by eight feet high, was made of beams and planks stolen about the dock in the night, and nailed to the piles of the wharf. It was above the waves of the highest tides, and was carpeted with a stove and utensils for cooking, and straw beds. The pantry was well filled with tea, sugar, bacon, bread, potatoes, and other edibles, and the boys, fifteen of whom regularly ate and slept there, were evidently good providers. The harbor police destroyed with ruthless hands this interesting house, which must have been cooler, if not healthier than many water-place residences, and took three boys, whom they caught, to a reformatory institution."

★ ★ ★

"Two fatal cases of cholera have occurred at Taylor's Barracks, Louisville, among the recruits recently arrived from New York. The cholera is still on the increase in New York. There were 62 cases on Blackwell's Island on the first. The weather is very warm, and considered favorable for the development of the seeds of the epidemic. Twenty-six cases and six deaths were reported in New York on the second. Nine new cases, two of them fatal, were reported to the Philadelphia Board of Health."

★ ★ ★

"A correspondent writes from Montana territory that there is no city in the country more quiet than Helena, and adds 'We have an active vigilance committee, plenty of rope, and a pine tree handy, where justice is laid at the time. There have been seven men hung on that tree.' "

★ ★ ★

"A despatch from Fort Laramie, states that the promised era of Indian murder and outrage has commenced. Thirty-five men are reported to have been massacred at Fort Conner. The herds belonging to government and private ranch men are suffering severely from their raids. The troops ordered forward by the government, for the defense of the frontier will arrive none too soon."

★ ★ ★

"The people of Milwaukee are a good deal excited by reason of a big swindle just practiced on them by a grand gift enterprise which has been flourishing in that town for some time under the firm name of 'Ludlum, Hale, and Company.' One hundred thousand tickets were to be sold at one dollar each, and the grand prize was advertised at $10,000 with numerous smaller ones. Seventy-five thousand tickets had been sold when the managers suddenly reached the conclusion that it would pay best to leave, and they did it, since which nothing has been discovered."

★ ★ ★

"A considerable emotion was created among the clerks in the departments at Washington on the discovery that the Civil Appropriation bill which passed Congress did not increase their pay 20 percent as it was supposed."

★ ★ ★

"Henry Ward Beecher has lately been pitching into practice of working railroad conductors on Sunday. The other day Mr. Beecher, in his peculiar way, was making inquiries of a conductor, to whom he was unknown, as to whether the Sunday riding could not be broken up.

" 'I think it might be,' said the conductor, 'but for that confounded Beecher. So many fancy people from all parts visit his establishment that it makes the road profitable. If he would only shut up, the thing could be done.' "

★ ★ ★

"A woman whose minor son was fleeced out $750 by gamblers on a Mississippi steamboat recently sued the captain of the boat and recovered the money. Judge Busteed, of the United States District Court in southern Alabama, in rendering the decision, declared that a gambler was a nuisance, and that it was the duty of a captain to protect his passengers and especially minors, from all such cormorants."

★ ★ ★

"Antioch College, at its late commencement, would not allow Mrs. S. W. Dodds (a graduate) to read her essay, because she wore a bloomer dress."

★ ★ ★

"The proposition made to send from California a section of the 'Original Big Tree' to the World's Fair at Paris, is said by Dr. Maggowan to be impractiable for want of a saw long enough to cut it. The cutting will require a saw 40 feet long."

★ ★ ★

"The President has issued his proclamation appointing the 29th day of November as a day of national thanksgiving and praise for the manifold blessings vouchsafed to us during the past year."

★ ★ ★

"A woman has just died at Portland, Maine, at the age of 70 who, for 35 years, has not spoken a loud word, in accordance with a vow she made on being disappointed in love."

★ ★ ★

"A lady correspondent of a Providence paper computes that if the women would cut their dresses to escape the ground one inch, instead of trailing two inches, as now the fashion, a saving of $1,000,000 would be annually effected. Here is a change for 'dress reform,' as well as for improvement in neatness."

★ ★ ★

"Mr. Gilbert, formerly governor of lower California, has been authorized by an imperial decree of Maximilian to establish a mint in that province. He has a privilege of fifteen years, at the end of which he must give to the state his whole establishment, without any remuneration."

★ ★ ★

"The number of deaths from cholera in St. Louis during the rage of the epidemic from about the first of August to the latter part of September, was over three thousand five hundred."

251